THE ROYAL COURT THEATRE PRESENTS

REAL CLASSY AFFAIR

by Nick Grosso

First performed at the Royal Court Theatre Upstairs
West Street, WC2 on 14th October 1998

Sponsored by the Jerwood Foundation

JERWOOD
NEW PLAYWRIGHTS

The Royal Court is delighted that the relationship with the Jerwood Foundation, which began in 1993, continues in 1998-99 with a fourth series of Jerwood New Playwrights. The Foundation's commitment to supporting new plays by new playwrights has contributed to some of the Court's most successful productions in recent years, including Sebastian Barry's **The Steward of Christendom**, Mark Ravenhill's **Shopping and F£££ing** and Ayub Khan-Din's **East is East**. Recent Royal Court productions supported by the Jerwood Foundation have received great acclaim and extended lives: Martin McDonagh's **Beauty Queen of Leenane** won Tony Awards in New York, Conor McPherson's **The Weir** is transferring to Broadway in 1999 and Jez Butterworth's **Mojo** is now playing at a cinema near you. This season the Jerwood Foundation continues to support vital, new theatre with Nick Grosso's **A Real Classy Affair**.

The Jerwood Foundation is a private foundation, dedicated to imaginative and responsible initiatives supporting young talent. In addition to sponsorships such as the Jerwood New Playwrights, the Foundation has just opened the Jerwood Space, a new arts centre in central London offering low-cost rehearsal and production facilities for young drama and dance groups and art gallery space for emerging artists.

The Beauty Queen of Leenane
by Martin McDonagh (Photograph: Ivan Kyncl)

The Weir by Conor McPherson
(Photograph: Pau Ros)

East is East by Ayub Khan-Din
(Photograph: Robert Day)

Mojo by Jez Butterworth
(Photograph: Ivan Kyncl)

REAL CLASSY AFFAIR
by Nick Grosso

Cast in order of appearance

Tommy Jason Hughes
Harry Callum Dixon
Joey Jake Wood
Billy Joseph Fiennes
Stan Nick Moran
Louise Liza Walker

Director James Macdonald
Designer Rob Howell
Lighting Designer Alan Burrett
Production Manager Paul Handley
Stage Manager Jo Cooper
Deputy Stage Manager Sandra Grieve
Costume Supervisor Alistair McArthur
Set Construction Robert Knight Ltd

The Royal Court Theatre would like to thank the following for their help with this production:
Wardrobe care by Persil and Comfort courtesy of Lever Brothers Ltd; refrigerators by Electrolux and Philips Major Appliances Ltd; kettles by Morphy Richards; video for casting purposes by Hitachi; backstage coffee machine by West 9; furniture by Knoll International; freezer for backstage use supplied by Zanussi Ltd 'Now that's a good idea.'; Closed circuit TV cameras and monitors by Mitsubishi UK Ltd; Natural spring water from Aqua Cool, 12 Waterside Way, London SW17 0XH, tel. 0181-947 5666; Overhead projector from W.H. Smith; backstage microwave supplied by Sanyo U.K; Watford Palace Theatre.

THE COMPANY

Nick Grosso (writer)
For the Royal Court: Sweetheart, Peaches.
Other theatre includes: Mama Don't (a monologue produced by the Royal Court Young People's Theatre and performed at the Commonwealth Institute in 1993).
Writer in Residence at the RNT Studio 1995 and 1996.
Film includes: The Art of Business.
Currently working on adapting Peaches as a feature film script.

Alan Burrett (lighting designer)
For the Royal Court: The Three Sisters (nominated for an Olivier Award).
His designs for theatre, opera and dance include the English National Opera, Royal Opera House Covent Garden, Los Angeles Opera, Geneva Opera, San Diego Opera, Munich Opera, Paris Opera, the Royal Danish Opera, the Royal National Theatre and many productions for the Royal Shakespeare Company. He also lit the Earls Court Arena versions of Tosca, the Duran Duran World tour and the complete Beckett Plays at the Lincoln Center Festival in New York. He has designed sets and costumes for the Béjart's Ballet and the Comédie Française's Tricentinary.

Callum Dixon
For the Royal Court: Faith, Mojo, Young Writers' Festival.
Other theatre includes: The Day I Stood Still, The Wind in the Willows, Somewhere, The Recruiting Officer, Rosencrantz and Gildenstern Are Dead (RNT); Edward II, Richard III, Two Shakespearian Actors, Bright and Bold Design (RSC); Accrington Pals, Mowgli's Jungle (Octagon Theatre, Bolton); All I Want to Be is An Ugly Sister (Lilian Baylis Theatre); Waiting at the Water's Edge (Bush Theatre); Macbeth (British Actors' Co UK tour); Woyzeck (RNT Studio); Deadwood (Watermill Theatre).
Television includes: The Queen's Nose, The Bill, The Knock III, The Tomorrow People, Hetty Wainthrop Investigates, April's Fool.
Film includes: Waterlands.
Radio includes: The Wolfgang Chase.

Joseph Fiennes
Theatre includes: Troilus and Cressida, The Herbal Bed, As You Like It, Les Enfants du Paradis, Son of Man (RSC); A View From the Bridge (West End, Bristol Old Vic & Birmingham Rep); A Month in the Country (Albery); Woman in Black (Fortune).
Television includes: The Vacillations of Poppy Carew.
Film includes: Shakespeare in Love, Elizabeth I, Martha Meet Frank Daniel and Laurence, Stealing Beauty.
Radio includes: Romeo and Juliet, Up Against It.

Rob Howell (designer)
For the Royal Court: Simpatico.
Other theatre includes: Snow Orchid, Salvation (Gate); Relative Values (Chichester Festival, national tour & Savoy); Eurovision (Sydmonton Festival & Vaudeville); Oliver! (Crucible, Sheffield); Private Lives (Dalateatern, Sweden); Julius Caesar (Royal Exchange, Manchester); True West, Peter Pan (West Yorkshire Playhouse); The Loves of Cass Maguire (Druid Theatre Company); Tartuffe, The Government Inspector (Almeida); Habeas Corpus, The Glass Menagerie, The Fix, How I Learned to Drive (Donmar Warehouse); Tom and Clem (Aldwych); Eddie Izzard - Glorious (Pola Jones); The Shakespeare Revue, The Painter of Dishonour, Little Eyolf, Richard III (RSC); Chips With Everything (RNT).

Jason Hughes
Theatre includes: Nothing to Pay (Thin Language Theatre Company, Cardiff & BAC); Macbeth (Theatr Clwyd); The Unexpected Guest (Theatre Royal, Windsor); A Slice of Saturday Night (Theatre Auf Tournee); Badfinger (Donmar Warehouse); The Illusion (Royal Exchange, Manchester); Snake In the Grass (Old Vic); The Herbal Bed (RSC & tour).
Television includes: Mature Adults, This Life, King Girl, Casualty, Strangers In the Night, Cyw Haul, Castles, The Bill, Peak Practice, London's Burning.
Radio includes: A Clockwork Orange.

James Macdonald (director)
For the Royal Court: Cleansed, Bailegangaire, Harry and Me, The Changing Room (Royal Court Classics), Simpatico, Blasted, Peaches, Thyestes, The Terrible Voice of Satan, Hammett's Apprentice, Putting Two and Two Together.
Other theatre includes: Roberto Zucco (RSC); Love's Labours Lost, Richard II (Manchester Royal Exchange); The Rivals (Nottingham Playhouse); The Crackwalker (Gate); The Seagull (Sheffield Crucible); Neon Gravy (RNT Studio); Miss Julie (Oldham Coliseum); Juno and the Paycock, Ice Cream & Hot Fudge, Romeo and Juliet, Fool for Love and Savage/Love, Master Harold & the Boys (Contact Theatre); Prem (BAC, Soho Poly).
Opera includes: Wolf Cub Village, Night Banquet (Almeida Opera); Oedipus Rex, Survivor From Warsaw (Royal Exchange/Halle); Lives of the Great Poisoners (Second Stride).

Nick Moran
Theatre includes: The Rivals (West End & Chichester Festival); Billy Liar (Salisbury Playhouse); The Beggars Opera (Belgrade, Coventry); Blood Brothers (West End); The Broken Jug (Edinburgh Festival).
Telivision includes: Thief Takers, Hope I Die Before I Get Old, Growing Pains, Casualty, Heartbeat, The Silent Lodger, Redemption.
Film includes: Long Time Dead, Lock Stock & Two Smoking Barrels, Miss Monday, The Future Lasts a Long Time, Clancy's Kitchen, Don't Be Afraid, Hard Days Hard Nights, Buddy's Song.

Liza Walker
Theatre includes: Closer (RNT & Lyric).
Television includes: Sisters, Casualty, Teenage Health Freak, Redemption, The Good Guys, Boon, Inspector Morse, Minder, Maigret, 99-1, Sab, Jo Brand - Through the Cakehole, Thief Takers, Holding On, The Grand.
Film includes: The Mad Monkey, Buddy's Song, Century, Jungle Book, Solitaire for Two, E=MC2, Hackers, Savage Play.

Jake Wood
Theatre includes: The Day I Stood Still, Chips With Everything (RNT); Serving It Up (Bush); Our Boys (Cockpit, Derby Playhouse & Donmar Warehouse); I Thought I Heard A Rustling (Theatre Royal, Stratford East).
Television includes: Gobble, Trial and Retribution, Holding On, Thin Blue Line, Casualty, It Could Be You, Eleven Men Against Eleven, A Touch of Frost, Bramwell, The Governor, A Breed of Heroes, The Bill, Murder Most Horrid, Red Dwarf (series 8).
Film includes: Dad Savage, Crime Time, Skulduggery, Revolution, Flesh and Blood.

THE ENGLISH STAGE COMPANY AT THE ROYAL COURT THEATRE

The English Stage Company was formed to bring serious writing back to the stage. The first Artistic Director, George Devine, wanted to create a vital and popular theatre. He encouraged new writing that explored subjects drawn from contemporary life as well as pursuing European plays and forgotten classics. When John Osborne's Look Back in Anger was first produced in 1956, it forced British theatre into the modern age. In addition to plays by 'angry young men', the international repertoire included Bertolt Brecht, Eugène Ionesco, Jean-Paul Sartre, Marguerite Duras, Frank Wedekind and Samuel Beckett.

The ambition was to discover new work which was challenging, innovative and of the highest quality, underpinned by a contemporary style of presentation. Early Court writers included Arnold Wesker, John Arden, Ann Jellicoe, N F Simpson, Edward Bond and David Storey. They were followed by David Hare, Howard Brenton, Caryl Churchill, Timberlake Wertenbaker, Robert Holman and Jim Cartwright. Many of their plays are now modern classics.

Many established playwrights had their early plays produced in the Theatre Upstairs including Anne Devlin, Andrea Dunbar, Sarah Daniels, Jim Cartwright, Clare McIntyre, Winsome Pinnock, Martin Crimp and Phyllis Nagy. Since 1994 there has been a succession of plays by writers new to the Royal Court, many of them first plays, produced in association with the Royal National Theatre Studio with sponsorship from the Jerwood Foundation. The writers include Joe Penhall, Nick Grosso, Judy Upton, Sarah Kane, Michael Wynne, Judith Johnson, James Stock, Simon Block and Mark Ravenhill. Since 1996 the Jerwood New Playwrights Series has supported new plays by Jez Butterworth, Martin McDonagh and Ayub Khan-Din (in the Theatre Downstairs), and by Mark Ravenhill, Tamantha Hammerschlag, Jess Walters, Conor McPherson, Meredith Oakes and Rebecca Prichard (in the Theatre Upstairs).

Theatre Upstairs productions regularly transfer to the Theatre Downstairs, as with Ariel Dorfman's Death and the Maiden, Sebastian Barry's The Steward of Christendom (a co-production with Out of Joint), Martin McDonagh's The Beauty Queen Of Leenane (a co-production with Druid Theatre Company), Ayub Khan-Din's East is East (a co-production with Tamasha Theatre Company). Some Theatre Upstairs productions transfer to the West End, such as Kevin Elyot's My Night With Reg, Mark Ravenhill's Shopping and Fucking (a co-production with Out of Joint) and Conor McPherson's The Weir.

1992-1998 have been record-breaking years at the box-office with capacity houses for Death and the Maiden, Six Degrees of Separation, Oleanna, Hysteria, The Cavalcaders, The Kitchen, The Queen & I, The Libertine, Simpatico, Mojo, The Steward of Christendom, The Beauty Queen of Leenane, East is East, The Chairs and The Weir.

Now in its temporary homes, the Duke of York's and Ambassadors Theatres, during the refurbishment of its Sloane Square theatre, the Royal Court continues to present the best in new work. After four decades the company's aims remain consistent with those established by George Devine. The Royal Court is still a major focus in the country for the production of new work. Scores of plays first seen at the Royal Court are now part of the national and international dramatic repertoire.

The Royal Court Theatre is financially assisted by the Royal Borough of Kensington and Chelsea. Recipient of a grant from the Theatre Restoration Fund & from the Foundation for Sport & the Arts. The Royal Court's Play Development Programme is funded by the A.S.K. Theater Projects. Supported by the National Lottery through the Arts Council of England. Royal Court Registered Charity number 231242.

AWARDS FOR THE ROYAL COURT THEATRE

Death and the Maiden and Six Degrees of Separation won the Olivier Award for Best Play in 1992 and 1993 respectively. Hysteria won the 1994 Olivier Award for Best Comedy, and also the Writers' Guild Award for Best West End Play. My Night with Reg won the 1994 Writers' Guild Award for Best Fringe Play, the Evening Standard Award for Best Comedy, and the 1994 Olivier Award for Best Comedy. Sebastian Barry won the 1995 Writers' Guild Award for Best Fringe Play, the 1995 Critics' Circle Award and the 1997 Christopher Ewart-Biggs Literary Prize for The Steward of Christendom, and the 1995 Lloyds Private Banking Playwright of the Year Award. Jez Butterworth won the 1995 George Devine Award for Most Promising Playwright, the 1995 Writers' Guild New Writer of the Year Award, the Evening Standard Award for Most Promising Playwright and the 1995 Olivier Award for Best Comedy for Mojo. Phyllis Nagy won the 1995 Writers' Guild Award for Best Regional Play for Disappeared.

Michael Wynne won the 1996 Meyer-Whitworth Award for The Knocky. Martin McDonagh won the 1996 George Devine Award, the 1996 Writers' Guild Best Fringe Play Award, the 1996 Critics' Circle Award and the 1996 Evening Standard Award for Most Promising Playwright for The Beauty Queen of Leenane. Marina Carr won the 19th Susan Smith Blackburn Prize (1996/7) for Portia Coughlan. Conor McPherson won the 1997 George Devine Award, the 1997 Critics' Circle Award and the 1997 Evening Standard Award for Most Promising Playwright for The Weir. Ayub Khan-Din won the 1997 Writers' Guild Award for Best West End Play, the 1997 Writers' Guild New Writer of the Year Award and the 1996 John Whiting Award for East is East. Anthony Neilson won the 1997 Writers' Guild Award for Best Fringe Play for The Censor. The Royal Court was the overall winner of the 1995 Prudential Award for the Arts for creativity, excellence, innovation and accessibility. The Royal Court Theatre Upstairs won the 1995 Peter Brook Empty Space Award for innovation and excellence in theatre.

At the 1998 Tony Awards, The Beauty Queen of Leenane (co-production with Druid Theatre Company) won four awards including Garry Hynes for Best Director and was nominated for a further two. The Chairs (co-production with Theatre de Complicite) was also nominated for six awards. This year Taormina Arte awarded the European prize New Theatrical Realities to the Royal Court for its efforts in recent years to discover and promote the work of young British dramatists.

THE ROYAL COURT THEATRE BOOKSHOP

Located in the foyer of the Duke of York's Theatre, St Martin's Lane, the Royal Court Theatre bookshop is open most afternoons and evenings until after the evening performance. It holds a wide range of theatre books, playtexts and film scripts - over 1,000 titles in all. Many Royal Court Theatre playtexts are available for just £2. Among these are the recent productions of:

The Old Neighborhood - David Mamet, Gas Station Angel - Ed Thomas, Yard Gal - Rebecca Prichard, Been So Long - Che Walker, Cleansed - Sarah Kane, I Am Yours - Judith Thompson, The Chairs - Eugène Ionesco, Never Land - Phyllis Nagy, Blue Heart - Caryl Churchill, The Censor - Anthony Neilson, East is East - Ayub Khan-Din, The Leenane Trilogy (The Beauty Queen of Leenane, A Skull in Connemara, The Lonesome West) - Martin McDonagh, Shopping and Fucking - Mark Ravenhill

The bookshop also sells polo shirts, record bags, mugs and chocolate. Telephone enquiries can be made directly to the Bookshop Manager, Del Campbell, on: 0171 565 5024.

THE ROYAL COURT NEEDS YOUR SUPPORT

The Royal Court Theatre, Sloane Square, was built in 1888 and is the longest-established theatre in England with the dedicated aim of producing new plays. We were thrilled to be awarded £16.2 million in September 1995 - from the National Lottery through the Arts Council of England - towards the complete renovation and restoration of our 100-year old home. This award has provided us with a unique opportunity to rebuild this beautiful theatre and building work is well underway at the Sloane Square site. However, in order to receive the full Lottery award, the Royal Court must raise almost £7 million itself as partnership funding towards the capital project.

The support of individuals, companies, charitable trusts and foundations is of vital importance to the realisation of the re-building of the Royal Court Theatre and we are very grateful to those who have already made a major contribution:

BSkyB Ltd, Double O Charity, Granada Group Plc, News International Plc, Pathé, Peter Jones, Quercus Charitable Trust, The Rayne Foundation, RSA Art for Architecture Award Scheme, Basil Samuel Charitable Trust, The Trusthouse Charitable Foundation, The Garfield Weston Foundation, The Woodward Charitable Trust

Our campaign to re-build the Royal Court Theatre, Sloane Square, is meeting with tremendous success: on-site, exciting transformations are now taking place. All work below ground has now been completed and, with the roof being laid on our new bar area underneath Sloane Square, a significant point in the development programme has been reached. Meanwhile, the Stage Hands campaign - which was launched with the aim of raising over £500,000 from audience members and the general public, towards our £7 million target - has also passed a major milestone. We've now raised over £300,000 in donations and pledges and we are grateful to our many supporters who have so generously donated to the appeal.

However, we still have some way to go to reach our goal and each donation keeps the building work at Sloane Square moving forward: for example, a donation of £20 pays for 40 bricks, a donation of £50 pays for cedar panelling for the auditorium and a donation of £100 pays for two square meters of reclaimed timber flooring. If you would like to help, or for further information, please contact the Royal Court Development Office on 0171 565 5050.

ROYAL COURT DEVELOPMENT COMMITTEE

PATRONS

The Royal Court (English Stage Company Ltd) is supported financially by a wide range of private companies and public bodies and earns the remainder of its income from the Box Office and its own trading activities.

The company receives its principal funding from the Arts Council of England, which has supported the Court since 1956. The Royal Borough of Kensington & Chelsea gives an annual grant to the Royal Court Young People's Theatre and the London Boroughs Grants Committee contributes to the cost of productions in its Theatre Upstairs.

Other parts of the company's activities are made possible by sponsorship and private foundation support: 1993 saw the start of its association with the A.S.K Theater Projects of Los Angeles, which is funding a Playwrights Programme at the Royal Court. 1997-98 marked the fourth Jerwood Foundation Jerwood New Playwrights series, supporting the production of new plays by young writers. 1997-98 also saw the Barclays New Stages - Staging the New season, with four productions and a stage design conference promoting the exploration of innovation in form and staging.

We are grateful to all our supporters for their vital and on-going commitment.

TRUSTS AND FOUNDATIONS
The Campden Charities
Sir John Cass's Foundation
The Esmée Fairbairn
　Charitable Trust
Paul Hamlyn Foundation
The Jerwood Foundation
The John Lyons' Charity
Peggy Ramsay Foundation
Alan & Babette Sainsbury
　Charitable Fund
Foundation for Sport & the Arts
The John Studzinski Foundation
The Wates Foundation

SPONSORS
AT&T
Barclays Bank plc
The Granada Group plc
Marks & Spencer plc
The New Yorker
Business Members
AT&T (UK) Ltd
British Interactive Broadcasting
BSkyB Ltd
Channel Four Television
Chubb Insurance Company of
　Europe S.A.
Davis Polk & Wardwell
Deep End Design
Goldman Sachs International
Heidrick & Struggles
Lambie-Nairn
Lazard Brothers & Co. Ltd
Mishcon de Reya Solicitors
OgilvyOne
Sullivan & Cromwell
J Walter Thompson
Tomkins plc

PRIVATE SUBSCRIBERS
Patrons
Advanpress
Associated Newspapers Ltd
Bunzl plc
Citigate Communications
Greg Dyke
Homevale Ltd
Laporte plc

Lex Service plc
Barbara Minto
New Penny Productions Ltd
Noel Gay Organisation
Anthony Perrins
A T Poeton & Son Ltd
Greville Poke
Richard Pulford
Sir George Russell
The Simkins Partnership
Simons Muirhead and Burton
Richard Wilson
Benefactors
Bill Andrewes
Batia Asher
Elaine Attias
Larry & Davina Belling
Jeremy Bond
Katie Bradford
Julia Brodie
Julian Brookstone
Guy Chapman
Yuen-Wei Chew
Carole & Neville Conrad
Conway van Gelder
Coppard Fletcher & Co.
Lisa Crawford Irwin
Curtis Brown Ltd
David Day
Robyn Durie
Winston Fletcher
Claire & William Frankel
Nicholas A Fraser
Norman Gerard
Henny Gestetner OBE
Carolyn Goldbart
Frank & Judy Grace
Sally Greene
Jan Harris
Angela Heylin
André Hoffman
Chris Hopson
Juliet Horsman
Institute of Practitioners
　in Advertising
International Creative
　Management
Peter Jones
Catherine Be Kemeny

Thomas & Nancy Kemeny
KPMG
Sahra Lese
Lady Lever
Collette & Peter Levy
Mae Modiano
Pat Morton
Joan Moynihan
Sir Alan and Lady Moses
Paul Oppenheimer
Michael Orr
Sir Eric Parker
Carol Rayman
Angharad Rees
B J & Rosemary Reynolds
John Sandoe (Books) Ltd
Nicholas Selmes
David & Patricia Smalley
Max Stafford-Clark
Sue Stapely
Ann Marie Starr
Richard Turk
Elizabeth Tyson
Charlotte Watcyn Lewis

AMERICAN FRIENDS
Patrons
Miriam Blenstock
Tina Brown
Caroline Graham
Richard & Marcia Grand
Edwin & Lola Jaffe
Ann & Mick Jones
Maurie Perl
Rhonda Sherman
Arielle Tepper
Members
Monica Gerard-Sharp
Linda S. Lese
Yasmine Lever
Leila Maw Strauss
Enid W. Morse
Gertrude Oothout
Mr & Mrs Frederick Rose
Mrs Paul Soros

FOR THE ROYAL COURT THEATRE

DIRECTION
Artistic Director Ian Rickson
Director Stephen Daldry
Assistant to the
Artistic Director Nicky Jones
Associate Directors Elyse Dodgson
James Macdonald
Max Stafford-Clark*
Trainee Director Janette Smith **
Associate Director Casting Lisa Makin
Casting Assistant Julia Horan
Literary Manager Graham Whybrow
Literary Associate Stephen Jeffreys*
Resident Dramatist Rebecca Prichard+
International Administrator Aurélie Mérel

PRODUCTION
Production Manager Edwyn Wilson
Deputy Production Manager Paul Handley
Head of Lighting Johanna Town
Senior Electricians Alison Buchanan
Lizz Poulter
Assistant Electricians Marion Mahon
Head of Stage Martin Riley
Senior Carpenters David Skelly
Christopher Shepherd
Terry Bennett
Head of Sound Paul Arditti
Sound Deputy Rich Walsh
Production Assistant Sue Bird
Costume Deputies Neil Gillies
Heather Tomlinson

YOUNG PEOPLE'S THEATRE
Artistic Director Carl Miller
Youth Drama Co-ordinator Ollie Animashawun
Outreach Co-ordinator Stephen Gilroy
General Manager Aoife Mannix
Writers' Tutor Noel Greig

ENGLISH STAGE COMPANY
President Greville Poke
Vice President Joan Plowright CBE
Council
Chairman Sir John Mortimer QC, CBE
Vice-Chairman Anthony Burton
Members Stuart Burge CBE
Stephen Evans
Sonia Melchett
James Midgley
Richard Pulford
Nicholas Wright
Alan Yentob

Advisory Council Diana Bliss
Tina Brown
Allan Davis
Elyse Dodgson
Robert Fox
Jocelyn Herbert
Michael Hoffman
Hanif Kureishi
Jane Rayne
Ruth Rogers
James L. Tanner

MANAGEMENT
Executive Director Vikki Heywood
Assistant to the
Executive Director Diana Pa
General Manager Diane Borger
Finance Director Donna Munday
Finance Officer Rachel Harrison
Re-development
Finance Officer Neville Ayres
Finance & Administration
Assistant Eric Dupin

RE-DEVELOPMENT
Project Manager Tony Hudson
Deputy Project Manager Simon Harper
Assistant to Project Manager Monica McCormack

MARKETING
Head of Marketing Stuart Buchanan
Marketing Officer Emily Smith
Press for *Real Classy Affair* Sally Lycett
(tel: 01424 225140)
Publicity Assistant Peter Collins
Box Office Manager Neil Grutchfield
Acting Deputy
Box Office Manager Valli Dakshinamurthi
Box Office Sales Operators Glen Bowman
Clare Christou
Jane Parker
Carol Pritchard*
Michele Rickett*

DEVELOPMENT
Development Director Caroline Underwood
Assistant to
Development Director Ruth Gaucheron
Head of Development Joyce Hytner*
Sponsorship Manager Helen Salmon
Trusts and Foundations Susan Davenport*
Development Assistant Sophie Hussey
Admistration Assistant Terry Cooke

FRONT OF HOUSE
Acting Theatre Manager Tim Brunsden
Deputy Theatre Manager Sarah Harrison
Acting Deputy Theatre Manager Jemma Davies
Duty House Manager Gini Woodward*
Relief Duty House Managers Neil Grutchfield*
Marion Doherty*
Bookshop Manager Del Campbell
Bookshop Supervisor Gini Woodward*
Maintenance Greg Piggot*
Lunch Bar Caterer Andrew Forrest*
Stage Door/Reception Lorraine Benloss*
Charlotte Frings
Tyrone Lucas*
Nettie Williams*
Benjamin Till*
Tom Hescott*
Cleaners *(Theatre Upstairs)* Maria Correia*
Mila Hamovic*
Peter Ramswell*
(Theatre Downstairs) Avery Cleaning Services Ltd
Firemen *(Theatre Downstairs)* Myriad Security Services
(Theatre Upstairs) Datem Fire Safety Services

Thanks to all of our bar staff and ushers

Royal Court Theatre
St. Martin's Lane, London, WC2N 4BG
Tel: 0171 565 5050 Fax: 0171 565 5001
Box Office: 0171 565 5000
www.royal-court.org.uk

* =part-time
+ =Arts Council Resident Dramatist
**=This theatre has the support of the Harold Hyam
Wingate Foundation under the Regional Theatre Young
Director Scheme administered by Channel 4.

Nick Grosso
Real Classy Affair

faber and faber

First published in 1998
by Faber and Faber Limited
3 Queen Square London WC1N 3AU

Typeset by Country Setting, Woodchurch, Kent TN26 3TB
Printed in England by Intype London Ltd

© Nick Grosso, 1998

Nick Grosso is hereby identified as author
of this w   ~f the
Cop

All rights   ed.
Applicati   r
including   ice,
prior to any   gency,

31
No perf   s

A CIP record for this book
is available from the British Library

ISBN 0-571-19592-X

2 4 6 8 10 9 7 5 3 1

Characters

Tommy 29
Harry 25
Joey 25
Billy 29
Stan 29
Louise 22

This text went to press before opening night.
There will, therefore, be differences between
the text and the play on the stage.

Real Classy Affair was first performed at the Royal
Court Theatre Upstairs on 14 October 1998 with the
following cast:

Tommy Jason Hughes
Harry Callum Dixon
Joey Jake Wood
Billy Joseph Fiennes
Stan Nick Moran
Louise Liza Walker

Director James Macdonald
Designer Rob Howell
Lighting Designer Alan Burrett

Part One

*North London pub. Identical suits and slicked-back
short hair. Tommy sports snakeskin shoes. Pints of lager.
Untouched whisky chasers.*

Tommy so anyway i goes . . .

Harry yeh?

Tommy i goes . . .

Harry yeh?

Tommy checks.

Tommy what did i go?

Joey i can't remember

Tommy i goes . . .

Joey and Tommy click fingers and point at each other.

Joey and Tommy that's right!

Tommy shakes his head.

Tommy i can't believe i said that

Harry *what*!?

Joey look there's billy

*The boys turn round and see Billy approaching.
Different colour suit. They start coughing.*

Tommy billy

Billy tommy

Billy nods.

5

boys

Harry billy

Billy how ya doing?

Tommy just the same . . . how about you?

Billy nods.

Billy likewise

Tommy this is a surprise

Billy is it? why?

Tommy b/cos you're a *stranger* . . . b/cos we never *see* you . . . that's *why* . . . why dya *think*?

Billy i dunno

Tommy b/cos you're never *around*

Billy i been busy

Tommy of *course* you have . . . we *know* you have . . . we *all* have let's face it . . . if you ain't busy these days what are ya . . . hey . . . ? nothing . . . you're *nothing* . . . and you ain't nothing billy no . . . you're more than that . . . ain't he boys?

The boys nod.

Harry definitely

Billy b/cos . . .

Tommy what?

Billy if i ain't welcome . . .

Tommy what?

Billy you know . . .

Tommy no i *don't* know

Billy i'll split

Tommy what?

Billy vanish

Joey vamoosh

Harry scarper

Billy peddle along

Tommy you won't peddle anywhere my friend will he boys?

The boys shake their heads.

Joey no way tommy

Harry never

Tommy you see

Tommy holds out his arm.

now put your peddles away and sit down

Billy where?

Tommy grab a pew . . . joey fetch the man a pew

Joey looks around.

Joey where?

Tommy i dunno look for one

Joey walks off. Tommy gives Billy Joey's stool.

there now sit down

Billy cheers

Billy sits down.

Tommy what's the matter with you? 'if i ain't welcome' . . . of *course* you're welcome . . . you're *always* welcome . . . you know that

7

Billy well i'm a bit sensitive

Tommy of *course* you are . . . we *know* you are . . .
you're a little *butterfly* that's what you are . . . you got
feelings . . . you're not like the rest of these fucking
elephants . . . that's why i like ya

Billy is it?

Tommy for *sure* . . . you're not thick-skinned like the
rest of these monkeys

Tommy points at Billy.

that's a rare gift in a man you know . . . in a woman you
expect it . . . they don't walk around like bleeding rhino-
ceroses do they . . . ? bumping into things . . . no . . .
they're more commendable . . . but in a man . . . well . . .
we're different ain't we . . . ? we're more . . . what's the
word . . . ?

Harry manly

Tommy yeh . . . we got more . . .

Tommy flexes his muscle.

manliness

Billy i dunno

Tommy no?

Billy i went out with this bird . . .

Tommy oh yeh?

Billy she was . . .

Billy's hands express her fulsome figure.

Harry i bet she was

Billy she was

Harry she weren't called sandra was she?

Billy jeremy

Harry looks shocked.

Harry what?

Billy it came as a bit of a shock

Harry i bet it did

Billy a bit of a fright

Harry you're damn right

Billy i went white

Harry i'm not surprised

Tommy looks dumbstruck.

Tommy shit

Billy you wanna get out more tommy . . . it's a crazy
world out there

Tommy nods.

Tommy i hear ya

Joey returns with a stool.

Joey here i found one

They look round at Joey.

this woman had her handbag on it – i said excuse me
love is this seat taken? – she said not right now no –
i said well i'm *talking* about right now ain't i i'm not
talking about bleeding tomorrow! – she had fear in her
eyes – she said i'm waiting for my husband – i said i
don't care if you're waiting for king bloody tutu . . . !
she started crying poor dear

Harry she didn't?

Joey she did – she thought i was gonna hit her

Harry looks shocked.

Harry what?

Joey she thought i was one of these wife-beaters or something – i said listen lady do i look the sort who dishes it out cos he ain't got a chair?

Harry what did she say?

Joey she was shaking – she was looking at my fists – i had em clenched – i didn't even *realise* – i was standing there with my fists clenched and she was about ninety-two and she had holes in her shoes and she was waiting for her ol fella – so i bought her a drink – she was shaking her *tits* off – she thought i was gonna *kill* her – i told her i ain't a *murderer* woman – she'd watched too many crime shows – so i got her a gin and tonic – slice of lemon – she looked *chuffed* – i said when your hubby comes you get me and i'll get him a chair – she was well chuffed – she thought i was mother teresa – she said he likes a pint of guinness – i said i'll get him a *chair* not a flaming *drink* you cheeky bitch – i tell ya these ol biddies – you gotta be careful – show em the slightest bit of kindness and they take libs – *libs* i tell ya – still i don't expect he'll show – not in this weather – he's probably crawled up in some corner dying of hypothermia

Harry nods.

Harry it's bitter out

Billy i blame the government

Harry for what?

Billy they shouldn't charge old folk for heating

Harry that's true

Billy not in this cold

Joey still they gotta die somehow

Harry death . . .

They stare at Harry.

it's part of life innit

Tommy to what do we owe this pleasure?

Tommy and Billy stare at each other.

Billy what?

Tommy joey get billy a drink will ya?

Joey of course

Tommy billy?

Billy that's very nice . . . i'll have a scotch

Tommy with ice?

Billy straight

Tommy joey get billy a scotch . . . large . . . no ice . . . i'll have the same

Joey walks off.

so?

Billy looks at Tommy inquiringly.

Billy what?

Tommy how come you're here?

Billy nods.

Billy oh that's nice innit?

Tommy what is?

Billy that is . . . very welcoming

Tommy well where have you been?

Billy i been busy – i said

Tommy yeh you said . . . with what?

Billy with all *manner* of things . . . who *cares* . . . ? so long as i'm here *now* hey

Tommy looks dubious.

Tommy i suppose

Billy who cares where the crow flies so long as it spreads its wings

Tommy you what?

Billy where the tiger roams

Tommy yeh yeh alright

Billy where the orangutan swings its limbs

Harry you been at the zoo billy?

Billy it *is* a fucking zoo harry

Billy points outside.

out *there* . . . it's a fucking *jungle* . . . a lion's *den*

Harry a spider's *web*

Billy shakes his head.

Billy it ain't pleasant

Joey returns with four whiskies and puts them down. Billy grins gleefully.

now *this* is pleasant

Joey puts his change down on the table. Tommy picks it up and hands it to Joey.

Tommy joey put that in the jukebox

Joey walks off.

so you're back now are ya?

Billy nods.

Billy yeh and i'm here to stay

Tommy well in that case . . .

Tommy raises his glass.

we'll drink to your health

The boys clink glasses.

your health squire

Billy cheers

Harry cheers

Joey's choice comes on. Frank Sinatra. They lean back and listen to him. Joey returns.

Joey some woman was standing with her son

Harry where?

Joey by the jukebox . . . she had him in her arms . . . he could only have been . . . what . . . ? five

Harry so?

Joey they shouldn't let kids in pubs

Harry why not?

Joey it ain't right

Billy i blame the government

Joey for what?

Billy the licensing laws

Harry what about em?

Billy it's ridiculous innit?

Harry what is?

Billy everything . . . the state of the nation . . . we're going down the *pan* . . . ! if i go the pub i wanna sit down . . . right . . . ? have a drink – listen to the juke-box – chat with my *mates* for christ sake – i don't want no five year old *cunt* pissing and shitting in my beer

Harry you what?

Billy yeh

Joey that's a bit strong

Billy *is it* . . . !? if i want kids i'll fucking have em – if i want a quiet drink i *won't* and i hope my local feels the same . . . ! you can't have tiny little tots tittering about sticking sherbert in your ale can ya . . . !? slobbering all over your custom-made clobber . . . bollocks!

Joey it's a bad influence

Billy points at Joey.

Billy precisely

Joey they'll end up on the piss

Harry so what?

Joey stares at Harry.

Joey how old are you harry?

Harry twenty-five

Joey and how old will you be next year?

Harry twenty-six

Joey and the year after?

Harry twenty-seven

Joey you see

Harry what?

Joey you're wasting your *life* away that's what!

Harry fuck off!

Joey it's *obvious* . . . ! twenty fucking seven and look at ya!

Harry what *about* me!?

Joey you're a fucking *mess* . . . ! you've done shit you know shit you look like shit

Billy leave it out joey

Joey i'm talking about *you* as well

Billy you what?

Joey i'm talking about *all* of us . . . not you tommy

Tommy thanks

Joey no the rest of us

Billy why's tommy exempt?

Joey he's different

Billy how?

Joey he just is

Harry you've been away billy you've missed a lot of things

Billy what things?

Joey tommy's been making waves

Billy has he?

Harry he's a big splash these days

Billy is he?

Billy stares at Tommy.

well?

Tommy i don't like to brag

Billy brag away

Tommy you know me

Billy i thought i did

Tommy modest as humble pie

Billy be bashful

Tommy i been active . . . let's say . . . in your absence

Billy it transpires

Tommy i been alive

Billy why what have you been doing?

Joey you'd know if you'd been around wouldn't ya?

Billy well there's some things *i* know that *you* don't

Harry oh yeh?

Billy nods.

Billy i got news

Harry what news?

Billy whose round is it?

Tommy joey get the drinks in

Joey okay

Tommy four of the same

Joey nods.

great

Joey walks off. Tommy stares at Billy.

Tommy well?

Billy it's about stan

Tommy what about him?

Billy he's leaving

Tommy where?

Billy here . . . he's moving to streatham

Tommy looks bemused.

Tommy what for?

Billy his nan's got a place there

Tommy she's dead

Billy i know . . . it's lying empty . . . it needs tending

Tommy he can hire a cleaner

Billy it ain't that

Tommy what is it?

Billy he *wants* to get out . . . he's *tired* of round here

Tommy stan?

Billy yeh

Tommy *tired*?

Billy yeh

Tommy of round here!?

Billy nods. Tommy shakes his head.

nah not stan

Billy i'm telling ya

Tommy nah . . . there's gotta be more to it

Joey returns with four whiskies and puts them down.

Joey that barmaid's a right dish you seen her?

They look round at the barmaid.

Harry janice?

Joey jan*eece*

Harry that's it

Joey a right sort . . . i goes can i have four shorts she goes you can i goes is that right she goes it is i go that's nice she goes what me or the drinks?

Harry she never?

Joey she did

Harry the tart

Joey i know . . . i'm going out with her friday

Harry you what?

Joey straight up . . . it's her night off . . . we're going the pictures

Harry to see what?

Joey one of them comedy romantics

Harry you asked her out?

Joey she practically asked *herself* out the tart . . . she had her tits in my face and all sorts . . . her lipstick . . . a right sauce

Billy what is it with you joey?

Joey what?

Billy wherever you go you always have a story

Joey do i?

Billy yeh

Joey thinks about it.

Joey it's cos i talk to people

Billy is it?

Joey i like people

Billy points outside.

Billy what them out there!?

Joey i like having a rapport

Billy a bit of banter

Joey yeh

Billy a bit of the other

Joey sometimes i smile sometimes i sneer

Billy it's all a veneer

Joey points at Billy.

Joey no it ain't superficial billy

Billy ain't it?

Joey no . . . it's genuine

Billy points at Joey.

Billy that's cos you're a genuine fella . . . a real top bloke

Joey i ain't nothing special billy am i tommy?

Tommy frowns.

Tommy nah

Billy but you *are* joey . . . you got a way with people

Joey grins.

Joey dya reckon?

Billy nods.

Billy it's a gift

Joey well if it is i was born with it

Billy let me tell ya something joey

Joey nods.

in all walks of life . . . right?

Joey nods.

there's different ways of doing things . . . un*told* ways in fact . . . but they all boil down to one thing

Joey what's that?

Billy 'the personal touch'

Billy points at Joey.

and you got it

Joey grins.

Joey dya reckon?

Billy i do

Joey well i've always been a personal chap

Billy you have . . . ever since we was kids . . . remember that time we went skating on the lake . . . and you fell in?

Joey chuckles.

Joey yeh

Billy and it was *freezing* . . . i had to fish you out?

Joey that's right

Billy points at Joey.

Billy remember?

Joey nods.

that was personal

Joey was it?

Billy for a five year old kid . . . !?

Joey when you put it like that

Billy points at Joey.

Billy i saved your life you scoundrel

Joey thanks billy

Billy everything you have you owe to me

Joey thanks billy

Billy when you bang that barmaid on friday night you'll know who to thank won't you?

Joey you

Billy when she's down on the floor on all fours and you're porking her from behind you know something joey?

Joey what's that?

Billy *i'll* be there with you

Joey steady *on* . . . !

Billy and you know why don't you?

Joey shakes his head.

Joey not a clue

Billy b/cos our lives are forever entwined

Joey you what?

Billy points at Joey.

Billy our fates are entrenched my friend don't forget that

Joey i won't

Billy that's why i'm sitting here and so are you . . . living . . . *breathing* . . . looking good

Joey dya want another drink billy?

Billy love one – thanks

Joey boys?

Tommy nods.

Tommy cheers joey

Joey walks off. Tommy stares at Billy.

so tell me

Billy looks at Tommy inquiringly.

about stan

Billy he's tired of the old faces

Tommy he can't be

Billy he is . . . believe me tommy he's changed

Tommy changed?

Billy had a phase . . . whatever . . . he ain't the same ol stanley

Tommy smirks.

Tommy fuck off

Billy he ain't

Tommy listen to me . . . will ya . . . please . . . ? i *know* stan and he ain't changed . . . the *weather's* changed . . . sure . . . the time of day . . . the presenter on the big breakfast . . . *they've* all changed

Tommy shakes his head.

not our stan

Billy you seen him lately?

Tommy course i have

Billy when?

Tommy what?

Billy when was the last time you saw him?

Tommy i don't *need* to see him i see him all the time

Billy when then?

Tommy harry when was the last time you saw him?

Harry looks vague.

Harry yonks ago

Tommy why?

Harry i dunno

Harry shrugs.

he ain't been around

Tommy well where's he been?

Harry i dunno

Harry shrugs.

wherever

Joey returns with four whiskies and puts them down.

Joey you'll never guess what's happened now?

Harry what?

Joey she's only got the hump with me in't she?

Harry who?

Joey janeece

Harry why?

Joey she says i was looking at her mate

Harry which one?

Joey the blond one

Harry was ya?

Joey *course* . . . she's a right sort

Harry what did she say?

Joey she said if i prefer her i can take *her* out

Harry so what's the problem?

Joey well i asked her out but she didn't wanna know

Harry when?

Joey last week

Harry she's playing hard to get

Joey i know

Harry go and pursue it

Joey i can't

Harry why not?

Joey that barman's got eyes for her

Harry so? we all have

Joey that's what *i* said . . . he only got *more* strung out then . . . he tried to bar me from the premises

Harry he never?

Joey he did . . . i told him . . . i said look son . . . he said my name's not son . . . i said look jack . . . he said my name's not jack

Joey opens his arms.

i said look whateveryourfuckingnameis . . .

Harry finicky cunt

Joey i know . . . i said she's only a rough ol tart

Harry a piece of british meat

Joey she ain't no fillet

Harry more a lump of lard

Joey i said she's not worth *fighting* over

Harry what did he say?

Joey he tried to smack me

Harry *what*!?

Joey turns out she's his sister

Harry looks shocked.

Harry no?

Joey straight up

Harry talk about keeping it in the family

Joey i know . . . i said look . . . jeff . . . andrew . . . whatever . . . mister 'ohverypleasantbarman' . . . when i said . . .

Harry 'tart'

Joey i didn't mean . . .

Harry 'tart'

Joey not in a condescending way

Harry no

Joey i meant it more as a term of . . .

Harry affection

Joey endearment

Harry a form of flattery

Joey points at Harry.

Joey exactly

Tommy joey when did you last see stan?

Joey checks.

Joey what . . . ? stan . . . ? oh . . .

Joey thinks about it.

not for a fair while tommy

Tommy why?

Joey shrugs.

Joey probably the same reason *you* ain't

Tommy why's that?

Joey i dunno

Joey shrugs.

sometimes you don't see people do ya?

Tommy sneers.

Tommy you lot are fucking great

Joey what's up?

Tommy he's one of your best *mates* for christ sake!

Joey so?

Tommy what's the matter with you?

Joey there's nothing wrong with *me* tommy i'm feeling great

Tommy you mean you haven't even called?

Joey thinks about it.

Joey no

Tommy you haven't even taken the trouble to pick up the phone and call?

Joey have *you*?

Tommy harry?

Harry shakes his head.

well i'm disappointed

Harry why?

Tommy i thought the least you could do is count on your *mates*!

Joey you *can*

Tommy evidently you *can't*!

Joey why not?

Tommy look at stan . . .

Joey what about him?

Tommy there he is . . .

Joey where?

Tommy a picture of despair

Harry points at Tommy.

Harry you don't *know* that tommy

Tommy of *course* i do . . . why else would he be moving to streatham?

Joey hey?

Tommy to live in his dead nan's flat . . . surrounded by her aura . . . it's not *right* . . . ! he must be in a pretty desperate way that's all i can say to wanna live *there* . . . to actually *wanna* live there . . . in streatham . . . rather than live *here* . . . where he's *always* lived . . . where he *knows* everyone . . . where everyone knows *him* . . . where they all know how he got that mark on his left leg the one he got when . . . you know . . .

Harry yeh

Joey perhaps he's tired of everyone knowing that

Tommy don't be *daft* . . . ! nobody *cares* . . . ! it's water under the *viaduct* . . . ! the only time someone mentions it is when it's hot and he wears his shorts and the sun brings it up and he has to put that cream on it . . . and besides . . .

Harry what?

Tommy he ain't the only one with a murky past is he billy?

Tommy and Billy stare at each other.

no something's happened

Harry what?

Tommy i dunno . . . but i'm gonna find out . . . joey give me some change

Joey what for?

Tommy just give me

Joey gives Tommy some change. Tommy gets up.

Harry what you doing?

Tommy i'm giving *stan* a call that's what i'm doing . . . i'm gonna show him that despite appearances his mates are still alive and still *think* about him from time to time that's what i'm doing . . . i'm gonna show him that when the chips are down and your back's against the wall and the shit has hit the fan and the fan has come un*stuck* and you're in *schtuck* . . . your mates'll pull you through

Tommy points at Harry.

that's what i'm doing

Harry gets up and holds out his hand.

Harry here give me that

Tommy what for?

Harry i'm doing what i shoulda done long ago . . . i'm calling stan

Tommy gives Harry the change.

Tommy good man

Harry imagine him there alone

Joey where?

Harry at home

Joey he lives with louise

Harry imagine him there with louise

Joey shit

Harry i know

Joey all alone with louise

Harry it's enough to drive anyone to streatham

Joey but he loves her

   Tommy smirks.

Tommy don't make me laugh

Joey what?

Tommy he dunno what love is!

Joey don't he?

Tommy *no* . . . ! he *thinks* he does . . . sure . . . we all do . . . but is it really love?

Joey bollocks

Tommy exactly

   Tommy points at Joey.

you said it joey . . . 'bollocks'

Harry *i* loved sally

Tommy you what?

   Harry looks indignant.

Harry i did

Tommy listen to him

Harry what?

Tommy '*i* loved sally' . . . you sound like gloria fucking hunniford . . . ! you loved *no-one* you just *thought* you did!

Harry is that right?

Tommy of *course* it is . . . ! thinking and being are two different things they're unrelated they ain't even *friends* . . . ! i mean *i* thought i was gonna play for arsenal didn't i?

Harry did ya?

Tommy when i was young . . . yeh . . . i couldn't even play for brentford . . . i thought mary was taking precautions that time we did it next to the arches remember?

Harry yeh

Tommy was she?

Harry no

Tommy stares at Harry.

Tommy no need to rub it *in* harry

Harry i'm just saying

Tommy no thinking only brings you grief . . . believe me . . . i've done a lot of thinking in my time . . . still do . . . all *sorts* of things

Tommy taps his temple.

it's my brain see . . . it won't switch off

Billy you wanna take it easy tommy . . . have a nice cup of tea

Tommy love . . . it ain't real . . . it's plastic . . . synthetic . . . it ain't a hundred per cent cotton . . . rip it up and it tears to shreds

Harry nods.

Harry that's what happened with sally

Tommy points at Harry.

31

Tommy you see

Joey gets up.

where you going?

Joey to phone stan

Billy get us a drink

Joey walks away.

Tommy joey

Joey turns.

Joey what?

Tommy raises his glass.

Tommy four of the same

Joey walks off.

well this is all a bit of a shock billy i must say . . . this
news of stan . . . i never knew he was so unhappy

Billy what's 'happy' tommy?

Tommy nods.

Tommy good point . . . still all the same . . . we all have
our off days i'll grant ya but . . . this is different . . . i
mean i've had my dark moments of course i have but
nothing so dark as to drive me to streatham . . . that's
positively pitch *black*!

Billy you know tommy i've often wondered

Tommy checks.

Tommy oh yeh?

Billy where were you when joey fell in?

Tommy what?

Billy the lake

Tommy where dya *think*?

Billy stares at Tommy.

Billy i'm stumped

Tommy making *plans*!

Billy for what?

Tommy the *celebration*!

Billy but he hadn't been *saved*!

Tommy but i never doubted your heroic potential billy not for a second

Billy perfectly understandable

Tommy opens his arms.

Tommy and what's a rescue without a wee celebration after?

Harry points at Tommy.

Harry that's you all over that is

Tommy what?

Harry always think ahead

Billy but there *was* no celebration joey ran off sobbing and didn't resurface for six *months*!

Tommy ahh but had he not he'd have had the party of his life and *why* harry?

Harry b/cos of *you* tommy

Tommy nods.

Tommy that's right

Harry you always do things in style

Tommy just as i'll do stan's send-off

Harry you what?

Tommy well if he's moving to streatham . . . as it appears he is . . . the least we can do is throw him a do . . . we may have neglected him of late but he'll have such a top night he'll forget he even *thought* of leaving

Billy don't worry it's all been arranged

Tommy and Billy stare at each other. Joey returns with four whiskies and a stool. He puts the drinks down.

Joey i phoned stan

Harry and?

Joey he weren't in . . . so i left a message saying 'stan it's joey'

Harry and?

Joey what?

Harry what else did you say?

Joey nothing the pips went . . . you took all my change

Harry sighs.

so anyway i bought the drinks and got some more and rang his mum

Harry what did *she* say?

Joey she weren't in either

Harry sighs.

but then a funny thing happened

Billy i thought it might

Joey it did . . . i put down the phone when i get this tap so i turns round and guess who it is?

Harry who?

Joey only the ol biddy's husband!

Harry who?

Joey remember the ol biddy with the handbag . . . ? the one who was shaking?

Harry oh yeh

Joey she'd sent him over to get me to get him a *chair* . . . ! course i didn't recognize him i'd never seen him before had i?

Harry no

Joey i didn't know him from adam but he introduces himself – i say great – nice to meet you and that – and then he goes can you get me a chair? – so i look around – i'm a bit flummoxed as you can imagine – a bit taken aback to say the least – i mean the last thing i expected was her to send him over in *my* whereabouts but i'd made a promise so i look around and there's not a spare chair in the house . . . not a poxy stool . . . nothing

Harry so what dya do?

Joey what i did was this – i gave him the drinks to hold onto – i said look after these – and then i went walkabouts – i came across a pair of lads with flop haircuts – you know the type

Harry yeh

Joey i said listen i know it sounds strange blah blah blah but there's this ol codger etcete*rar* only this time my fists are clenched and i'm *aware* so they get up and give me *both* their stools so i say no i only want one – just the one like – but they insist – so anyway . . . here it is

Joey holds up the stool.

the spare

Joey sits down on his stool and puts his feet up on the spare. He nonchalantly lights a cigarette. Tommy stares at Billy.

Tommy so it's all been arranged?

Joey what has?

Billy nods.

Billy it's on sunday

Tommy where?

Billy my place

Tommy your place?

Billy nods.

how come?

Billy well louise agreed . . . i volunteered and . . . everyone was happy

Tommy everyone?

Billy nods.

who?

Billy everyone . . . stan . . . stuart . . . the mob

Joey what's going on?

Billy a party

Joey what time should i get there?

Billy seven

Joey can i bring janeece?

Harry she's not talking to you remember?

Joey oh yeh . . . what about blondie?

Billy bring who you like

Tommy well listen billy the least i can do . . . seeing as it's at your yard and everything . . .

Tommy pulls out a wad of notes.

is help with the cost

Billy no it's alright

Tommy i insist . . . i mean if we're all gonna be there . . .

Billy that's just it

Tommy what is?

Billy you're not

Tommy checks.

Tommy what?

Billy gonna be there . . . you're not invited tommy

Tommy who says?

Billy stan . . . that's what i come to tell ya . . . there's a party sunday but you're not invited

Harry what about *me*?

Billy *you're* invited

Tommy you mean everyone's invited but me?

Billy nods.

Billy that's about the jist yeh

Tommy looks stunned.

i'm sorry tommy

Tommy any particular reason?

Billy there is in fact

Tommy what?

Billy the reason you're not invited tommy . . . is cos *you're* the reason he's leaving

Tommy looks taken aback.

Tommy me?

Billy nods.

what have i done?

Billy he won't say

Tommy well in that case . . .

Tommy pulls out his mobile.

i'll ask him myself

Tommy starts dialling.

Harry what are you doing?

Tommy calling stan

Harry he's not in remember?

Tommy oh yeh

Tommy stops dialling.

shit

Joey tommy if you've brought your mobile . . . ?

Tommy yeh?

Joey how come you make me use the pay phone?

Tommy cos i don't use it sundays do i?

Harry why not?

Tommy cos me mum says it's not right

Joey nods.

anyway where the fuck is he?

Tommy has an idea.

i'll try *his* mobile

Tommy starts dialling. Billy shakes his head.

Billy i wouldn't do that

Tommy why not?

Billy it's switched off

Tommy stops dialling.

Tommy how dya know?

Billy he's not taking any calls

Tommy why not?

Billy shrugs.

what's going on billy?

Billy shrugs.

Billy search me

Tommy what have you been saying?

Billy nothing

Tommy you've been turning him against me

Billy why would i do that?

Tommy i dunno

Billy you know your problem tommy?

Tommy what's that?

Billy you're paranoid

Joey no it's just his complexion

Billy you're like the guy on top of the hill . . . 'charlie big potatoes' . . . looking down on his flock . . . scared they're all talking about him . . . but the truth of the matter is . . . they got better things to do

Tommy nods.

Tommy how rural

Harry rustic

Joey don't be sarcastic

Tommy you tell stan . . . i don't *care* if he ain't taking my calls . . . you tell him i'll be round

Billy when?

Tommy tomorrow

Billy looks sceptical.

Billy i'll tell him tommy but he might not like it

Tommy i don't *care* if he fucking likes it . . . tell him i want him *there* . . . tell him we'll get this sorted

The boys sup their pints. Not a whisky has been touched.

SCENE TWO

North London flat. Ironing piled up to the ceiling. Louise is ironing in front of the TV. Pinny and slippers. Stan is sat in an armchair drinking a can of beer staring at the TV. Tie loosened. Shirt unbuttoned at the top. Boxers. Socks. He scratches his balls. Tommy stands just inside the doorway. Overcoat done up. Leather gloves. Snakeskin shoes.

Tommy well i've had better welcomes i must say . . . charming . . . 'nice to see you tommy' . . . 'sit down' . . . 'have a cup of tea or something stronger' . . . you'd think we were complete strangers!

Stan we almost are

Tommy nods.

Tommy oh that's nice innit . . . ? very cutting . . . very 'droll' stanley . . . i mean i've only traipsed halfway across town to visit you

Louise you live down the road

Tommy yes i *know* i live down the road louise . . . thank you . . . i *know* where i live . . . but i weren't at *home* though was i . . . ? no . . . i was at a drinking club up west

Stan which one?

Louise don't you mind which one

Tommy the one we went with ben

Stan oh yeh

Tommy very dapper . . . very 'post-modern chic' stan . . . people are making deals as we *speak*

Tommy pulls out his mobile.

they're trying to get through . . . but i'm switched off

Tommy holds out his mobile.

i've got it on my answer service

Louise smiles at Tommy ironically.

Louise i'm touched

Tommy so you should be it's not everyone i make sacrifices for but this is different innit i mean we're like *family*

Louise you're nothing *like* my family

Tommy no that's true they're all villains

Louise they're decent people thank you!

Tommy opens his arms.

Tommy well there you go the similarities *abound* . . . ! they positively *abound* louise . . . ! decent people with decent jobs and decent lifestyles . . . decent sets of teeth

Louise we coulda been doing anything

Tommy you what?

Louise when you burst in

Tommy like what?

Louise use your imagination!

Tommy stares at Louise.

Tommy at this hour!?

Louise you don't know

Tommy it's not even tea time!

Louise so?

Tommy well i'm sorry to break up the fucking orgy i didn't know this was a den of ubiquitous *sex* i thought you two were *married* for christ sake!

Louise and married people don't do that?

Tommy not with each other

Louise not in *your* book

Tommy well look i can pop out and come back in . . . what . . . ? twenty minutes . . . or dya like to shower after?

Louise smiles at Tommy ironically.

i mean seriously when did you two last do it?

Stan tommy

Tommy no hold on a minute

Louise glares at Tommy.

Louise you what?

Tommy well look at the pair of ya

Louise glares at Stan.

Louise what have you been saying?

Tommy stan and me *talk* louise we're old *mates* we played on the swings together

Tommy looks at Stan.

here remember them?

Stan yeh

Tommy looks at Louise.

Tommy there was three of em

Louise i don't care

Tommy green blue and . . .

Tommy looks at Stan.

Stan yellow i think

Tommy that's right

Stan how i loved that playground

43

Louise where's this?

Stan where we lived

Tommy course it ain't there now the council got rid

Stan tuts.

Stan flaming council

Louise stares at Stan.

Louise dya know that's the first political thing he's said since i've known him?

Tommy is it?

Louise yeh

Tommy opens his arms.

Tommy well there you *go* that's what my company *does* for him you see it *inspires* him it takes him to another *plane* . . . !

Louise looks bemused.

Louise what – talking about green swings?

Tommy points at Louise.

Tommy they may be mere green swings to *you* louise but to *us* they're . . .

Tommy looks at Stan.

what are they?

Stan memories

Tommy stares at Stan.

Tommy succintly put stan

Tommy nods.

'memories'

Tommy makes a banner with his hand

'memories of unbridled youth'

Stan i had my first snog in that playground

Tommy smirks.

Tommy we all did

Stan all with the same girl

Tommy stacy richards

Stan 'spacey stacy'

Tommy no it was *racey* stacy it was spacey *tracey*

Stan that's it

Tommy cor blimey she was dizzy

Stan not as dizzy as dizzy lizzy

Tommy i thought it was *lippy* lizzy?

Stan it was *busy* lizzy

Tommy that's it

Tommy and Stan clock each other.

Tommy and Stan so who was dizzy?

Louise er *excuse* me!

The boys look at Louise.

shall i leave!?

Tommy no you don't have to do that lou it's *your* flat

Louise thank you

Tommy *we'll* leave

Louise shakes her head.

Louise oh no you won't

Tommy why not?

Louise stan's stopping in tonight

Tommy are you?

Stan shrugs. Tommy looks at Louise.

we only want a quick jar

Louise shakes her head.

a wee dram

Louise shakes her head.

we've things to discuss

Louise stan's not talking to you are you stan?

They look at Stan.

well?

Tommy let me tell ya something lou

Louise smirks.

stan *always* talks to me i'm his best *man* we go back
years . . . before you was *born* even . . . he tells me
everything . . . if you knew what *i* knew about him . . .

Stan tommy

Tommy well let's just say you wouldn't see him as you
do now

Louise what does *that* mean?

Tommy raises his eyebrows.

stan what does *that* mean?

Stan ignore him

Louise i can't ignore him he's standing in *front* of me for christ sake how can i ignore him?

Stan pretend he's not there

Louise well where *is* he?

Stan i dunno pretend he's in monte carlo

Louise stares at Tommy.

Louise yeh but he's *not* in monte carlo though is he?

Stan pretend he is

Louise stares at Tommy.

Louise it ain't easy

Tommy tell her to pretend i'm somewhere else stan somewhere she's been i mean she's never been to monte carlo has she she can't imagine me there you've never taken her and why not?

Stan we can't afford it

Tommy no that ain't it she wouldn't enjoy it

Louise smirks.

Louise don't be daft

Tommy it's not your scene louise believe me you'd get there and find there's no baked beans and be back like a shot

Louise you what?

Tommy the hotel'd do your laundry and you'd be *bored*!

Louise looks at Stan.

Louise are you gonna just *sit* there?

Tommy you'd have nothing to do lou b/cos without your laundry . . .

Tommy taps his temple.

you're clueless

Stan leave it out tommy

Tommy you're like a sparrow in a cage full of kangaroos

Louise looks bemused.

Louise what?

Tommy 'lost'

Louise looks at Stan.

Louise is that all you can *say*?

Tommy of course it is you've drained the life outa him

They look at Stan slumped in his armchair clutching a can.

he's a shell of the man he was

Tommy looks around the drab room.

and it's all b/cos of this

Louise what?

Tommy opens his arms.

Tommy 'domesticity'

Tommy points at Stan.

you see that man there . . . he used to be the talk of the town

Louise when?

Tommy in the old days . . . 'finsbury's finest' he was

Louise looks at Stan.

Louise you never told me this?

Tommy that's cos he's ashamed

Louise of what?

Tommy the stunts he used to pull

Louise such as?

Tommy they was just high jinks louise

Louise all the same . . .

Tommy we was kindred flames

Louise who was?

Tommy we both was . . . sizzling through the swelter
like char-grilled romeos

Louise you what?

Tommy i jest not

Louise looks at Stan.

Louise is this true?

Stan he's over-romanticizing you know tommy

Tommy they'd make tracks for us

Louise who would?

Tommy your everyday joes . . . your common hybrids . . .
they'd sweep the street from under our feet and we'd
stroll through the mall like latter day kings

Louise pall mall?

Tommy of course

Louise you used to go there?

Tommy we was very particular

Louise how were the clubs?

Tommy of the highest order

Louise looks at Stan.

Louise how come you never take *me* there?

Stan frowns.

Stan nah

Louise why not?

Stan it's just people drinking . . . and dancing and joking

Stan frowns.

it ain't much cop

Louise it sounds a ball

Stan it's just folk having fun that's all

Louise looks at Tommy.

Louise will you hark at him

Tommy he's settled in his ways

Louise when i think of the days . . .

Tommy he's past that phase

Stan we've had our fun ain't we tommy?

Tommy we've had a crack

Louise when i think back . . .

Tommy no don't do that lou you'll just get depressed

Louise glares at Tommy.

Louise why will i?

Tommy you'll compare it to *now* i mean you're like an old woman in your pinny

Stan *i* bought that pinny

Tommy well that says it *all* dunnit!?

Stan what does?

Tommy there was a time when you mighta bought her saucy knickers but now you buy her a bleeding apron!

Stan she's *got* saucy knickers

Tommy and when does she wear em?

Louise that's none of your affair!

Tommy you may as well give em to *me i'm* more likely to fucking wear em!

Stan slams his can down on the coffee table and stands.

Stan that's it

Tommy what?

Stan you may be my oldest friend tommy . . .

Tommy opens his arms.

Tommy *me . . .* !? i thought i was a *stranger* remember . . . ? you're chumming it up with *billy* from what *i gather*!

Tommy and Stan stare at each other. Tommy smirks.

i mean billy

Louise points at Tommy.

Louise don't speak bad of billy tommy i'm warning you

Tommy looks surprised.

Tommy what's got your goat?

Louise oh yeh we're proper soul mates didn't he say?

Tommy looks flummoxed.

Tommy no he didn't

Louise well we've the time ain't we what with not working and his things being as they are

Tommy what things?

Louise his bits and bobs

Tommy what's those then?

Louise oh don't fret they're all legit

Tommy i'm glad to hear it

Louise no we've formed a sorta mutual bond

Tommy sneers at Stan.

Tommy and you know about this?

Louise oh he encourages it don't ya stan?

They stare at Stan.

Tommy well?

Stan it's all above board tommy

Louise oh there's nothing untoward it's just two people with time to kill chewing over things in a cafe perhaps or a little diner off the main road . . . away from the traffic . . . billy's not keen on traffic you see he thinks there should be more walkways

Tommy nods.

Tommy does he now?

Louise oh he's a sensitive thing when his guard slips

Tommy he's a little butterfly that's what he is

Louise i'm glad you agree

Tommy wholeheartedly louise

Louise we'll share a pot of tea and some devon creams and mull over the day's events

Tommy there must be *loads*

Louise oh there *are* tommy his days are *filled*

Tommy with what?

Louise all sorts

Tommy i never knew this?

Louise we'll have some pate . . . perhaps . . . duck liver . . . an aperitif . . . a spot of brandy

Tommy lovely

Louise whatever's on the menu oh he *pays* of course he's very giving

Tommy and Louise stare at each other.

not like some

Tommy well i must say stan i'm impressed

Stan with what?

Tommy your liberal attitude

Stan dya reckon?

Tommy i do you put me to *shame*

Stan how's that?

Tommy well i might get a tad jealous

Stan there's no cause

Tommy still you must be pretty trusting

Stan i suppose

Tommy letting louise loose like that

Stan i *want* her to know my mates tommy

Tommy stares at Stan. Long and hard.

Tommy say what?

Stan so we can all hang out

Tommy stares at Stan. Long and hard.

Tommy say what?

Stan without there being an atmosphere

Tommy stares at Stan. Long and hard.

Tommy what atmosphere?

Stan you mean you ain't noticed?

Tommy no

Stan well it may have passed you by but i'm acutely aware

Tommy of what?

Stan something in the air whenever lou's round

Tommy dya reckon?

Stan i do

Tommy well i'm staggered by your insight stan and there i was totally blinded

Stan of course it's all down to resentment

Tommy says who?

Stan professor of psychology

Tommy looks bemused.

Tommy do what?

Stan lou saw a show about it apparently he cited the beatles

Tommy why?

Stan well there they were at the top of their game when john met yoko and it all went pony

Tommy you can hardly blame *her* though

Louise precisely

Stan the rest got moody cos they felt neglected

Stan looks at Louise.

that's right innit love?

Louise nods.

Louise spot on

Stan now had she *integrated* more so this professor goes . . . you know mixed with the lads say . . . played pinball . . .

Stan opens his arms.

things mighta been different

Tommy is that so?

Stan it is

Tommy and lou told you this?

Stan she did

Tommy so you let her off her leash?

Stan nods.

Stan in a nutshell

Tommy well lucky ol billy hey?

Tommy nods.

i bet he's laughing no *end*

Stan he's not that way tommy

Tommy raises his eyebrows.

Tommy oh no?

Tommy and Stan stare at each other.

guess what he tried to do?

Stan when?

Tommy yesterday

Stan nods inquiringly.

only turn joey against me

Stan he never?

Tommy he flaming did!

Stan how?

Tommy he started talking about old times . . . when we was kids . . . on the lake

Stan so?

Tommy i see joey every day i look out for him

Louise do you heck

Tommy what does *he* fucking do . . . ? crop up in a blue moon and prattle on about how *close* they are!

Stan like you're doing *now* you mean?

Tommy looks taken aback.

Tommy oh that hurts that does stan . . . that really hurts . . . that hits me right . . .

Tommy puts his hand on his heart.

there

Louise they can reminisce

Tommy oh they can can they?

Louise yes!

Tommy you mean it's alright for them but not for us?

Louise what?

Tommy me and stan . . . we can't go out and think back

Louise not tonight no

Tommy besides he weren't reminiscing he was getting at *me*

Stan how dya mean?

Tommy he *knows* i can't skate!

Stan and Louise look bemused.

Louise you what?

Tommy shakes his head.

Tommy you don't understand

Stan you take things too *personally* tommy

Tommy points at Stan.

Tommy and that's another thing

Stan what?

Tommy he said joey was personal

Louise what does *that* mean?

Tommy it don't mean *shit*

Louise you *can't* be personal you can be a *person* but not *personal*

Tommy *exactly*!

Louise you can *talk* personal

Tommy that's what *i* said . . . lou . . . that's *exactly* what *i* said!

Tommy opens his arms.

he didn't get it

Tommy taps his temple.

he's thick . . . he ain't the full quota . . . stan pour us a drink will ya i'm gasping

Stan scotch?

Louise stan

Stan catches Louise's glare.

Stan you can't deny him a drink

Tommy you can't deny me a drink lou not after all that i mean i was best man at your flaming wedding!

Louise's glare eases. Stan walks towards the drinks.

here stan what about the speech?

Tommy chuckles.

was that a pucker speech or what?

Tommy catches Louise's glare.

yeh well maybe not

Louise it was crude

Tommy that weren't crudeness louise that was sardonic wit

Tommy catches Louise's glare.

okay it was crude . . . but was it funny . . . ? i mean did
they laugh?

Stan we're outa scotch

Tommy it took an *age* to write that speech i tell ya an
absolute *age* . . . i must spent . . . what . . . ? six weeks
on it . . . full-time

Louise six weeks to write a speech?

Tommy straight up . . . i mean first there was the
research i had to call all his ex . . .

Tommy catches Louise's glare.

i mean all his mates . . . and then there was the actual
writing of it the punctuation that was a well prepared
speech i dunno if you noticed there was a lot of little
nuances in it that added to it i mean a lot of little titbits

Louise glares at Tommy.

Louise i noticed

Stan here tommy we're outa scotch

Tommy what?

Tommy checks.

no?

Stan nods.

never?

Stan i'm sorry

Tommy what have i always said stan . . . ? hey?

Stan 'never run outa scotch'

Tommy that's right

Tommy points at Stan.

i've always said that you can't say i ain't

Stan you have

Tommy anything else you can do without . . . food . . . water . . . condoms . . . they're all surplus . . . but scotch is a basic human neccessity

Stan i'll pop down and get a bottle

Louise shakes her head.

Louise no you won't

Stan why not?

Louise let *him* go

Stan it's no bother

Tommy dips his hand in his pocket.

Tommy i tell ya what i'll cover it

Stan it's alright

Tommy pulls his hand back out.

i'll be back in a minute tommy sit down

Tommy pulls off his overcoat and gloves as Stan puts on his suit and shoes.

lou don't be rude to tommy after all he's my best man

Tommy i'm his best man

Stan that's gotta stand for something innit?

Tommy of course it has

Tommy has on the same suit as the previous scene. Stan's is the same colour. They are dressed identically. except for the shoes. Tommy puts his arm around Stan. They look at Louise.

i tell ya that was the perfect day your wedding

Stan weren't it just

Tommy the sun was shining the stars were out

Louise how could the sun be shining if the stars were out?

Tommy i'm just setting the *scene* louise no need to be picky

Louise sighs.

the registry office was *clean*

Louise of course it was

Tommy the birds were humming and lou looked a picture didn't she stan?

Stan nods.

Stan a picture

Tommy she looked like a goddess

Stan a princess

Tommy a prince of gods

Stan a god of princes

Louise alright cut it out

Louise can't help but smile.

Tommy that was the perfect day it really was and the reception oh and the *speech* . . . !?

Stan nods.

Stan it was good

Tommy it was more than *good* stan it was a flipping *masterpiece*!

Stan that's what i meant

Tommy i mean there's speeches and there's speeches and *that* was a speech believe me

Stan winks at Louise.

Stan i'll be back in a minute

Stan walks away.

Tommy oh and stan

Stan stops and turns.

Stan what?

Tommy get a single malt

Stan sighs.

Stan i'll have to go further

Tommy it's worth it innit?

Stan sighs.

Stan i suppose

Tommy take the car

Stan shakes his head.

Stan i sold it

Tommy looks taken aback.

Tommy you sold the saab?

Stan i had to

Tommy but you loved that car?

Stan i'm saving up

Tommy for what?

Stan i got plans tommy

Tommy oh yeh?

Stan big plans

Tommy well then you can walk

Louise dya know what a single malt *costs*?

Tommy dips his hand in his pocket.

Tommy i'll cover it

Stan no you're alright

Tommy pulls his hand back out. Stan and Louise clock each other.

i'll be back in a minute

Stan walks off. he is heard leaving the flat. Tommy stares at Louise. She continues ironing.

Tommy he's a diamond your fella

Louise is silent.

i tell ya they *broke* the mould

Louise is silent.

why did he sell the saab?

Louise is silent.

you need a car you can't rely on buses

Louise is silent.

listen lou if things are tight . . .

Louise they're not

Tommy i'll buy a new one

Louise smirks.

you what?

Louise is silent. Tommy nods.

oh that's nice innit i offer you a car and you call me mean

Louise well you are

Tommy it don't have to be a car . . . it can be anything . . . a dishwasher

Louise i've got one

Tommy a telly

Louise what's wrong with ours?

Tommy nothing

Tommy looks at the TV.

it's fine . . . is it a bit green?

Louise what?

Tommy the picture . . . it looks a bit green

Louise that's what stan says

Tommy perhaps it's the tube

Louise no there's no trains near here

Tommy no i mean the tube inside the telly

Louise oh

Tommy perhaps i can pay for a new one?

Louise looks up at the TV and frowns.

Louise i don't mind a bit of green

Tommy don't ya?

Louise no

Tommy why not?

Louise well say you're watching inspector morse and he's wearing a red shirt you think he's wearing a green shirt

Tommy do ya?

Louise or what do red and green make?

Tommy mauve

Louise well then there you go you think he's wearing a mauve shirt

Tommy and that amuse you does it?

Louise quite

Tommy frowns.

Tommy nah it's not right . . . i mean it's hardly becoming a chief inspector *that* . . . is it . . . ? a mauve shirt . . . !? all the crooks'd scoff

Louise they're all repeats anyhow

Louise continues ironing. Tommy looks at the TV and shrugs.

Tommy i suppose

Louise is silent.

listen lou can i ask you something?

Louise is silent.

are you pregnant?

Louise looks up at Tommy.

Louise you what?

Tommy i'm asking

Louise no i'm not

Tommy holds his hands up.

Tommy fine

Louise why dya say that?

Tommy is silent.

listen tommy what happened that time . . .

Tommy what about it?

Louise it was an error

Tommy i know

Louise i was tipsy and . . .

Tommy let's drop the subject hey?

Louise drops her head.

i weren't *talking* about that dya think i'd mention that in stan's flat?

Louise is silent.

stan's my mate i'm his best man

Louise you say that loads

Tommy well i am

Louise so why dya seduce his wife?

Tommy stares at Louise.

Tommy i never said i was uncomplicated

Louise sneers at Tommy.

Louise look at you

Tommy what?

Louise you've got the lot and yet you chase the one thing he has . . . the one thing he can turn to people and say that's mine

Tommy stares at Louise.

Tommy you're moving me

Louise sneers at Tommy.

Louise you should be ashamed

Tommy opens his arms.

Tommy but i'm not how dya fathom it?

Louise taps her temple.

Louise b/cos you live in a dark place

Tommy how's that?

Louise you're *cold* tommy you cut everyone off but yourself

Tommy nods.

Tommy it's true i'm the sole person i don't lie to

Tommy opens his arms.

is it a sin . . . ? i look at you and i see what i want i say 'tommy that's what you want don't deny it ol chum you're only lying to yourself and you know how the truth matters'

Louise smirks.

but *you* lou . . . you see me . . . and get scared

Louise nods.

Louise you've got it all sussed

Tommy i do my best

Louise i'll tell you about truth shall i?

Tommy if you must

Louise points at the door.

Louise the truth comes through that door every night after work tommy *that's* the truth . . . the truth brings home the bacon . . . not when it's flush or struck luck but each *month* . . . on the table . . . the truth i can look at on a morning . . . cook breakfast . . . fried eggs . . . the truth says my eggs are fine

Tommy the truth looks at you with these eyes lou

Tommy taps below his eye.

just remember how they look at you

They stare at each other. Louise tuts.

Louise i should be ironing

Louise continues ironing. Tommy watches her.

Tommy you know i do a bit sometimes

Louise looks at Tommy inquiringly. Tommy nods at the ironing.

when i have to

Louise i can't see it

Tommy i ain't that good

Louise it's a knack

Tommy i can *see* that

Louise is silent.

i mean i can see how you're meant to do it . . . when *you* do it or me *mum* . . . but when *i* try . . .

Tommy shakes his head.

it just don't come out right

Louise perhaps your heart's not in it

Tommy smirks.

Tommy perhaps

Louise is silent.

mind you i went to sparks the other day they got these creaseless shirts for twenty quid you seen em?

Louise is silent.

you just bung em in the dryer and presto

Louise if only life were so easy

Tommy it *is* . . . i mean it *can* be . . . i bought ten of em

Louise ten?

Tommy now every day i look spanking

Tommy pulls of his jacket and shows off his shirt. front and back. Louise looks up at him.

see

Louise can't help but smile. She nods.

Louise very nice

Tommy i said to the cashier i said surely if you buy ten there's a discount

Louise what did *she* say?

Tommy she just laughed . . . she thought i was charming her

Louise and was ya?

Tommy i was trying to get a discount

Louise nods.

Louise that figures

Tommy i ain't tight louise i'm just prudent

Louise what does *that* mean?

Tommy it means if you've got it flaunt it but don't give it away

Louise i'll remember that

Tommy yeh perhaps you should

> *Louise glares at Tommy.*

Louise i ain't a *tart* tommy if that's what you think?

Tommy i never said that

Louise it was a one-off

Tommy i thought we were off the subject

Louise we are

Tommy i asked her out

Louise who?

Tommy the cashier

Louise what was she like?

Tommy she was alright . . . she went to college she was part-time . . . she was one of these 'modern' women . . . she studied philosophy

Louise what did you talk about?

Tommy not much she was too intellectual

Louise what about philosophy?

Tommy i gave her *mine* alright

Louise i thought you might

Tommy i said if you stay up late and get up early you won't miss much

Louise what did *she* say?

Tommy she said she had a lecture in the morning
Tommy shakes his head.

silly cow

Louise never mind

Tommy she weren't my type anyhow
Louise raises her eyebrows.

Louise what's that?
Tommy opens his arms.

Tommy you know me lou i like the simple life
Louise smirks.

Louise yeh right

Tommy glass of wine

Louise i don't like wine

Tommy cottage pie

Louise i don't eat beef

Tommy slice of cheese

Louise i don't have dairy products
Tommy opens his arms.

Tommy you see we're made for each other
Louise frowns.

Louise they don't agree with me

Tommy is there anything you *do* like?
Louise thinks.

Louise sunday roast

Tommy but you don't eat beef?

Louise i skip the beef

Tommy oh

Louise and the tatties

Tommy no wonder you're anorexic!

Louise i'm just petite!

Tommy you're lovely

Louise stan says i'm gaining

Tommy let's see

> *Louise comes round the ironing board and shows Tommy her figure. Tommy admires her.*

you look great

> *Louise frowns.*

Louise i dunno tommy i feel a bit dowdy i wanna get my hair done i'm thinking of dying it

Tommy what colour?

Louise pink

> *Tommy stares at Louise.*

Tommy pink?

Louise yeh

Tommy you can't do that!

Louise why not?

Tommy you just can't!

Louise why not?

Tommy thinks.

Tommy you just can't

Louise you're too conservative you are

Tommy points at Louise.

Tommy i voted labour . . .

Louise i mean you're a stick in the mud

Tommy oh

Louise no i think pink'd look good

Louise looks at herself in the full-length mirror.

Tommy what's wrong with *your* colour?

Louise it's just not *me* tommy pink would show off my natural exuberance

Tommy your natural *what*?

Louise it would make me more bouncy

Tommy what's all this about lou?

Louise i wanna be *noticed* tommy

Tommy you *are* noticed

Louise shakes her head.

Louise i never get asked out

Tommy you what?

Louise well take that cashier . . . the student

Tommy what about her?

Louise was she a stunner?

Tommy looks vague.

Tommy she weren't exactly a stunner no

Louise what was she?

Tommy she was a dog

Louise but you still asked her out?

Tommy i ask everyone out you know me

Louise no-one asks *me* out

Tommy but you're *married*!

Louise blokes don't know that

Tommy of *course* they do you wear a *ring*

They stare at each other.

you mean you don't?

Louise smiles and shakes her head.

why you telling me this?

Louise shrugs.

why don't you tell billy i'm sure he'll be plenty
interested?

Louise is silent.

or a mate or dya have none of your own?

Louise glares at Tommy. She points at the phone.

Louise i'll have you know that phone never stops going i
have to take it off the hook just to get me chores done . . .

Tommy of course you do

Louise it's flipping frightening . . . i mean there i'll be
doing my thing when it rings and it's a friend wishing to
while away the hours well time's too precious innit i've a
life a rich and varied one i can't afford to idly gossip i
might catch rigor mortis

Tommy points at Louise.

Tommy i hope you tell em lou

Louise you bet i do i say 'i'm sorry sweetie i don't mean to be rude but i'm in the middle of shit you know couldn't i call you back . . . like next year'

Tommy oh lou you don't?

Louise smirks.

Louise i'd welcome the chance

Tommy what about your old gang?

Louise shakes her head.

Louise i've lost touch

Tommy but *why?*

Louise well when i started seeing stan . . .

Louise chuckles to herself.

Tommy what's up?

Louise shakes her head.

Louise i remember when i met him i thought i could *never* date a stan

Tommy why not?

Louise it's so old fashioned innit?

Tommy i suppose

Louise but he was such a *gent* tommy i mean *far* better than the blokes *i* knew they only wanted one thing

Tommy which was?

Louise what dya think?

Tommy so you fell for him?

Louise well i wouldn't say *that* exactly no

Tommy no nor would i

Louise glares at Tommy.

Louise but we got *on* well which *you'd* know nothing about

Tommy nods.

Tommy oh i know about getting on alright lou . . . oh yeh . . . no problem . . . to get on you gotta get up . . . first and foremost . . . bright and breezy . . . b/cos coming round that corner'll be the biggest gifthorse you've ever seen and if you ain't on your toes my cherub it'll canter off into the next garden and leave you *standing*

Louise nods.

Louise and that's you is it . . . ? come to save me?

Tommy opens his arms.

Tommy if you like

Louise you know why i like stan tommy?

Tommy why's that?

Louise he don't talk *shit* . . . he's dignified . . . he belongs to another world . . . one where people are honest

Tommy nods.

Tommy and so you moved in together?

Louise in part yeh

Tommy i see

Louise looks around the room and smiles.

Louise when we got the flat i was *so* made up tommy

Tommy i recall

Louise i was *so* content i neglected my friends *that's* what i'm *talking* about

Tommy well that happens

Louise i know

Tommy i mean if i told you the girls *i've* neglected

Louise what?

Tommy cos of my friends

Louise that's not what i meant

Tommy shakes his head.

Tommy it's diabolical

Louise anyhow they're all busy now

Tommy looks at Louise inquiringly.

my old gang

Tommy you can still call em

Louise shakes her head.

Louise they think i'm boring

Tommy who says?

Louise shrugs.

Louise i can feel it

They stare at each other.

Tommy well let's face it lou you *are*

Louise *what*!?

Tommy i mean look at you

Louise peers down at herself.

Louise what *about* me!?

Tommy you're twenty-one

Louise twenty-*two* thank you

Tommy i mean the blokes in the pub . . .

Tommy checks.

Louise what about em?

Tommy whenever your name crops up . . .

Tommy checks.

Louise what?

Tommy well they make fun of ya

Louise who does?

Tommy all of em

Louise who?

Tommy i dunno

Louise joey?

Tommy nah not joey don't be daft he *adores* ya

Louise harry?

Tommy not harry harry loves ya he's a *diamond*

Louise then who?

Tommy shrugs.

billy?

Tommy looks vague.

Tommy well . . .

Louise what did he say?

Tommy i don't wanna go into details

Louise go on

Tommy let's just say i didn't like it

Louise looks surprised.

Louise you mean you stuck up for me?

Tommy of *course* i did

Tommy points at Louise.

i told him straight i said look billy . . . if i hear one more word . . . i won't be responsible

Louise what did he do?

Tommy he shut up good and proper

Louise is this true?

Tommy of *course* it is

Louise you're not very subtle are ya?

Tommy what?

Louise smiles at Tommy.

Louise you're jealous we get on

They stare at each other. Tommy shakes his head and chuckles to himself.

Tommy that ain't billy you get on with lou oh no that's an altogether different person

Louise it *looks* like billy

Tommy nods.

Tommy sure . . . i'll grant ya . . . but when you meet the *real* one you'll know

Louise why?

Tommy he's hiding things from you

Louise like what?

Tommy just take my word for it

Louise well stan's not said nothing

Tommy stan only sees the good in people that's his trouble you can only spot your own and he's an honest sort as you rightly said and how's the world repay him?

Louise how?

Tommy it *spits* on him *that's* how

Louise he has a good life!

Tommy he works every hour god sends to support a wife who frolics with his friends . . . ! that's hardly being blessed is it?

Louise glares at Tommy.

Louise and for his sins he has a mate like *you* . . . tommy . . . one who won't cede until he's crushed

Tommy frowns.

Tommy harsh words lou

Louise but untrue?

Tommy to get what you want you gotta be despicable i don't make the rules i just *abide* by em

Louise *revel* in em even

Tommy shakes his head.

Tommy it ain't easy being me you know oh no i know you *think* it is

Louise my heart *bleeds*

Tommy there's downsides

Louise say *one*

Tommy when a man makes it all the way to the peak he finds there's no-one to join in the fun

Louise you feel lonesome?

Tommy we've more in common than you realise . . . louise . . . evidently . . . i mean i know by rights i'm free and you're enclosed . . . most certainly . . . but at the end of the day . . . we're both alone

They stare at each other. Long and hard.

Louise dya want a scotch?

Tommy looks bemused.

Tommy what?

A bottle of scotch appears. Louise grabs it. Tommy watches her.

shit

Louise pours two drinks.

you sneaky bitch

Louise hands Tommy a glass. He raises it to her.

cheers

They take a sip. Eyes fixed on each other.

lou that's mean

Louise is silent.

sending stan out like that

Louise is silent.

and now he's had to go further

Louise only cos you insisted

Tommy well i like a single malt

Louise smiles at Tommy.

Louise i recall

Louise stands back and shows Tommy her figure.

so you don't think i'm gaining?

Tommy admires her. He frowns.

Tommy nah

Louise stan thinks i am

Tommy what does *he* know?

Louise he sees me every day

Tommy but it depends *how* dunnit

Louise what dya mean?

Tommy well there's different ways of seeing things in't
there there's the way *stan* sees you . . .

Louise which is?

Tommy well let's face it lou he don't bat a lid

Louise's face drops.

and there's the way *i* see you

Louise perhaps you better shut up tommy

Tommy why?

Louise save you say something you regret

Tommy i don't regret i just remember

Louise well perhaps you oughta forget

Tommy it's the scotch lou it gets me all nostalgic

Tommy shrugs.

always has

Louise well i'll just have to put it away then

Tommy so you gonna have kids then tell me?

Louise looks startled.

Louise you what?

Tommy you heard

Louise that's none of your affair tommy

Tommy whose is it?

Louise mine and stan's

Tommy what does *he* say?

Louise we ain't discussed it

Tommy surely you've discussed it?

Louise no

Tommy how long have you been together?

Louise three years

Tommy since you was nineteen

Louise so?

Tommy well there comes a time when you gotta move on

Louise we *are* moving on

Tommy nods.

Tommy oh yeh that's right . . . i almost forgot . . . you're moving to . . .

Tommy clicks his fingers.

where was it?

83

Louise streatham

Tommy nods.

Tommy that's the one

Tommy smirks and sits down on the armchair. He grabs the remote and flicks through the channels. He undoes his collar and loosens his tie. He takes his shoes off and rubs his feet. Louise has returned to her ironing.

you know something lou?

Louise is silent.

all these cunts on the box

Louise what?

Tommy well

Louise then switch it off

Tommy nods.

Tommy that's your answer to everything

Louise is silent.

if there's a problem

Tommy changes channel.

press a fucking button

Louise is silent.

it's easier these days of course

Louise what is?

Tommy switching things off . . . there's always something to distract you

Louise like what?

Tommy like the washing

Louise tell me about it

Tommy you live in a vacuum

Louise that reminds me

Tommy what?

Louise the hoover's on the blink

Tommy are you *listening* to me!?

> *Louise puts down the iron and looks up at Tommy.*

i'm talking about *us*!

Louise there's nothing to discuss besides stan's back in a
minute

> *Tommy flicks through the channels. Louise continues
> ironing. Lights fade down. Spotlight on Tommy.*

Tommy i know this fella . . . he's got this remote pad . . .
it works the tv the telephone the fucking coffee maker . . .

Louise tommy

Tommy it's true . . . i was at his yard . . . with his son . . .
he's got a five year old son . . . little cunt he is

> *Louise glances up at Tommy.*

anyway we was watching the horses . . . it was a sunday
and a race was on . . . now i don't like the horses

Louise don't ya?

Tommy no . . . the others do . . . joey . . . harry . . .

Louise stan

Tommy they love em . . . i don't see the point

Louise why not?

Tommy i just don't . . . but if a race is on and i'm watching . . .

Tommy opens his arms.

well i like to see who wins

Louise of course you do

Tommy so we're watching this race and it's getting tighter . . . the horse on the inside is closing when . . .

Tommy pauses.

Louise what?

Tommy the little cunt turns over

Louise looks bemused.

Louise what?

Tommy just near the finishing line . . . he switches to bugs fucking bunny

Louise smiles.

Louise bless

Tommy so i give him a look

Louise i bet you did

Tommy i did and he turns back and it's over

Tommy opens his arms.

'over'

Tommy nods.

that's what fucking happens

Louise looks bemused.

Louise what are you *on* about?

Tommy i'm on about *simple* things!

Louise like *what*?

Tommy if you watch something you watch it to the *end* you don't change in the *middle* of it!

Louise kids might

Tommy that's just *it* it ain't just *kids* it's *everyone*!

Louise who?

Tommy *you* for instance!

Louise nods.

Louise i see

Tommy you think if i turn the box off *that* cunt'll go away

Louise who?

Tommy *him*

Tommy points at the TV.

that *green* cunt . . . jeremy beadle

Louise that ain't jeremy beadle

Tommy whoever . . . you think you can turn a blind eye . . . ! but you can't . . . ! he's there whether you watch him or not . . . prattling on

Tommy flicks the TV off.

talking shit

Louise shakes her head.

you wanna sweep things under the carpet but the thing about carpets is . . .

Louise isn't paying attention.

louise

Louise puts down the iron and stares at Tommy.

sooner or later they need airing

Tommy points at Louise like he's made a point. He flicks the TV back on and gazes at it. Louise stares at him. Lights come up.

Louise tommy you know your shirts?

Pause.

Tommy yeh

Louise you say you don't iron em?

Pause.

Tommy i don't they're creaseless

Louise so what *do* you iron?

Tommy looks bemused.

Tommy hey?

Louise dya iron your socks?

Tommy smirks.

Tommy don't be daft

Louise your strides?

Tommy i get a service wash they come back ready-pressed

Louise nods.

Louise i see

Tommy you know betty in the launderette?

Louise yeh

Tommy she does it for me

Louise that's nice

Tommy she don't charge me so i get her flowers . . . she says i shouldn't but then *she* shouldn't should she . . . ? i end up spending more on flowers than i would on laundry

Tommy chuckles to himself.

still

Louise i thought your uncle had a flower stall?

Tommy he has

Louise well?

Tommy i'm being hypothetical

Louise nods.

why dya wanna know anyway?

Louise i was just wondering

Tommy what?

Louise how come you're on your own

Tommy gets up to pour himself a refill.

i mean a bloke like you

Tommy what about me?

Louise well you're handsome

Tommy dya reckon?

Tommy admires himself in the mirror.

Louise you're resourceful

Tommy yeh i *am* a bit of a dish

Louise you're charming

Tommy looks taken aback. He turns to face Louise.

well kinda

Tommy yeh it's a fucking mystery innit?

Tommy walks up behind Louise and puts his glass down on the ironing board.

Louise i think it's a shame

Tommy why?

Louise well all those assets . . . they should be lavished on someone

Tommy grabs Louise's breasts from behind and fondles them.

Tommy like this?

Louise presses Tommy's hands tighter against her.

Louise tommy get off

Tommy moves a hand downwards.

tommy

Louise pulls his hand towards her crotch.

get off

They get into it. They knock the drink over and it spills over Tommy's trousers. He stands back and peers down at the damage.

Tommy shit!

Louise pulls him by the tie towards her.

Louise come here.

Tommy these cost a fortune!

Louise smirks.

what?

Louise shakes her head.

Louise that's typical

Tommy well

Louise take em off

Tommy looks surprised.

Tommy what?

Louise i'll fix em

Tommy stares at Louise.

take em off!

Tommy takes off his trousers and hands them to Louise. She walks off with them. Tommy picks up the glass and refills it. he sits down in the armchair and flicks through the channels. Gazes at the TV. Louise walks on and drapes the trousers over the side of the armchair. Tommy inspects them and seems satisfied. Louise goes over and wipes the drink from the carpet. She continues ironing.

you know something tommy?

Pause.

Tommy what's that?

Louise i think you're scared of intimacy

Tommy looks bemused. He turns to face Louise.

Tommy and what was that a minute ago?

Louise you're scared to show your inner feelings is what i mean

Tommy am i?

Louise yeh

Tommy what's brought this on?

Louise you're attracted to impossible situations cos deep down you don't *want* that situation

Tommy *what* situation?

Louise me and you

Tommy you're being a bit deep today?

Louise well it's all that daytime telly

Tommy who *says* i don't want it anyway not your professor again?

Louise shakes her head.

Louise you don't

Tommy it's only impossible cos *you're* moving and *why* are you moving?

Louise looks up at Tommy inquiringly.

b/cos you're *scared* i told you

Louise smirks.

Louise that ain't it

Tommy what then?

Louise stan's nan's flat

Tommy smirks.

it's bigger than here . . . it's free which means we might afford a car or . . .

Louise checks.

Tommy what?

Louise kids even

Tommy so you *do* want kids?

Louise of *course* i do!

Tommy and that's why you're saving up?

Louise no

Tommy what then?

Someone is heard entering the flat. Tommy and Louise stare at each other.

Louise i'll let stan tell you

Tommy turns to face the TV. Louise continues ironing. Stan shouts from off-stage.

Stan it's bloody *freezing* out there trust me to run outa scotch in a blizzard!

Stan walks on. He is wearing an overcoat and leather gloves. He resembles Tommy at the start of the scene. He is holding a bottle of scotch. He stares at the scene before him. Louise is ironing. Tommy is sat in the armchair gazing at the TV wearing only boxers, socks, shirt undone at the top, loosened tie. He is clutching a drink. He resembles Stan at the start of the scene.

what's all this . . . ?

Louise looks up.

Louise oh he spilt his drink daft thing

Stan notices the bottle of scotch.

Stan how . . . ?

Louise oh i found it in the cupboard

Stan looks bemused.

Stan funny i looked there

Louise it was right at the back

Stan shakes his head.

Stan that's typical

Stan points outside.

it's fucking *freezing*

Tommy and Louise chuckle. Louise continues ironing. Stan clears his throat.

anyway look who i bumped into

Billy walks on and stands beside Stan. Same overcoat. Same leather gloves. He nods at Tommy.

Billy tommy

Tommy and Louise's face drops. They face him. Billy nods at Louise.

louise

Louise smiles.

Louise billy this is a nice surprise how are you?

Billy it's like a holocaust out there

Louise what dya mean?

Billy i mean it's *cold* have you been out?

Louise shakes her head.

Louise not today no

Billy it's like a bleeding holocaust

Stan and Louise clock each other.

i saw stan carrying a bottle i thought 'aye aye what's going on' he goes tommy's upstairs i goes 'not my dear ol tommy *surely*' i mean fancy popping by the same night that's uncanny innit i ain't been here in *ages* how long in fact a fair ol whack and you louise you look lovely

Billy shakes his head.

don't she look lovely boys?

The boys look at Louise.

you look a million dollars in your pinny i *do* like that who got it?

Stan *i* did

Billy nods.

Billy very nice stan

Stan dya reckon?

Billy very C&A yeh

Billy looks at Louise closer.

are you pregnant by any chance?

Louise looks surpised.

Louise you what?

Billy you look a bit tubby

Louise glares at Billy. Billy chuckles and holds up his hands.

only kidding

Billy looks at Stan.

well do i get a drink or what?

Stan of course

Stan fetches Billy a drink. Billy takes his coat and gloves off. Different colour suit. Stan hands him his drink.

Billy cheers

Billy downs it in one.

well that warms the cockles i must say any chance of another?

Stan pours Billy a refill.

so how is everyone?

Louise fine

Billy i'm glad to hear it i'm alright myself you know me i don't complain i could if i wanted but where does it get you hey nowhere

Stan have a seat billy

Billy cheers

Louise glares at Stan. Billy sits down on the sofa. Takes off his coat. His suit is the same colour as previous scene. He surveys the flat.

it's nice in here stan have you decorated?

Stan no

Billy it doesn't show

Louise completes the ironing.

Louise well that's me done

Billy so tell me tommy what you been up to i hear you're a bit of a boy these days?

Tommy frowns.

Tommy not really

Billy nods and clocks Stan.

Billy always the coy bloody beggar weren't he?

Billy clocks Tommy.

have you heard about this restaurant?

Stan bistro

Billy that's it . . . stan's been chewing my ear off has he told you?

Tommy looks at Stan.

Tommy no not yet

Billy it sounds a pucker move

Stan dya reckon?

Billy i do there's a shortage of bistros only the other day i was looking for somewhere to eat and you get tired of the same old thing you want a bit of *variety* in your diet that's what i say you can't live on chinese *alone* you need a bit of something different something to tickle your taste buds something with a bit of *flavour* to get you through the cold weather . . . seaweed's meant to be good but i've never had the balls to try it

Louise has finished packing up.

Louise i'm off to bed

The boys turn to face Louise.

Billy so early?

Louise i'm bushed billy

Stan see you love

Billy yes ta-ta louise

Louise clocks Tommy.

Louise it was nice to see you tommy

Tommy nods.

Tommy and you

Louise come and visit us in streatham

Tommy i will

Lights fade down. Spotlight on Tommy. He watches Louise walk off. Billy winks at Tommy.

Billy aye aye

Tommy what?

Billy you two are very close

Tommy what dya mean?

Billy i'd watch my back if i were you stan

Stan what's that?

Billy tommy and louise

Stan i thought she had the hump with you?

Tommy you know lou she's a softy

Stan looks surprised.

Stan is she?

Tommy so tell me about this bistro?

Stan it's a blinding place tommy i saw it and i *knew* i had to have it

Billy points at Stan.

Billy that's instinct that is *always* trust your instinct

Stan i am

Billy hang about and you'll miss the boat

Stan i won't

Billy taps his nose.

Billy the early bird and all that

Tommy have you been drinking?

Billy i've had a few why?

Tommy you were saying?

Stan it's always been an ambition tommy

Tommy you never said?

Stan well you woulda *laughed* at me

Billy points at Stan.

Billy now that's unfair that is stan

Stan dya reckon?

Billy i do tommy's always been good to you

Stan who says?

Billy *he* does

Tommy but why a bistro?

Stan it's one of them things tommy . . . some kids wanna be fireman i wanted to have a bistro . . . well in those days it was a chain of restaurants

Tommy but why now?

Stan why not?

Tommy frowns.

Tommy it's a tricky business

Billy no it's not you'll be *rolling* in it a little bit of houmus for starters

Stan exactly

Billy some taramasalata for afters . . . vanilla ice cream . . .
it can't fail

Stan what dya reckon for the decor?

Billy nods.

Billy oh you'll need some decor stan that's for sure

Stan no i mean what *style*?

Billy stares at Stan.

Billy i'd go continental

Stan would ya?

Billy nods.

Billy definitely

Stan why?

Billy to make people forget they're in england

Stan looks bemused.

Stan why dya wanna do that?

Billy points outside.

Billy have you been out lately?

Stan yeh

Billy then you know

Stan know what?

Billy know england is on its *knees*!

Stan looks bemused.

Stan it's just a bit *cold* that's all

Billy stan this land is going to the *dogs* and when it *does* the few lucky punters in your bistro will survey the continental decor and have a *lot* to thank you for believe me

Tommy and Stan clock each other. Billy grabs the bottle and holds it out.

boys?

Tommy and Stan nod and Billy pours three drinks. He fills the glasses to the top. The song 'Like a Woman' by the Tony Rich Project plays. Spotlight goes down.

Part Two

*North London pub. Suits. Joey, Harry, and Stan sport a
new colour. So does Billy. Again his is different. Pints of
lager. Joey walks on with the shorts.*

Joey is it me?

Harry what?

Joey i seem to have an affinity with barmaids

Harry how dya mean?

Joey well take that darling over there

The boys look round.

Harry the brunette?

Joey Linda's her name

Harry yeh?

Joey she gives me my drinks and says is that all i say yeh
she says never mind i say why what was on offer?

Harry you never?

Joey i did

Harry you saucy git

Joey she says come after closing and find out

Harry now that's a touch

Joey i know

Billy it's definitely you joey

Joey grins.

Joey dya reckon?

Billy you got a way with people i told you

Stan i could with some of that around the bistro

Harry are you offering him a job?

Stan perhaps

Joey i can't cook stan

Stan you don't have to

Joey i can pour drinks

Stan that might be useful

Joey i can show people in and take their coats and see if they fancy any hors d'oeuvres

Harry like a concierge?

Joey nods.

Joey now you read me

Stan i tell ya what i'll have a think about it

Joey well don't take too long i might get other offers

Billy looks curious.

Billy here stan tell me something

Stan what?

Billy what's it like being the boss?

Stan i ain't the boss *yet* billy

Harry but you will be?

Stan i will be and when i *am* i'll tell ya

Billy will there be a party?

Stan looks at Billy inquiringly.

for the opening

Stan nods.

Stan there'll be a few drinks laid on yeh

Joey can i bring my baby?

Stan looks at Joey inquiringly. Joey nods towards the barmaid. Stan chuckles.

Stan if you like

Joey she'll be well chuffed . . . i'll give her the once over tonight and tomorrow i'll say my mate stan's got himself a bistro and he's having a do and i'd like *you* to be my escort

Joey shakes his head.

she'll be well chuffed

Billy looks over at the barmaid.

Billy she ain't a bit common?

Joey you what?

Billy i mean we don't wanna lower the tone

Joey what tone?

Billy i mean now stan's a restauranteur

Joey a what?

Billy he's in the bistro business

Joey oh

Billy he's his image to think of

Joey what image?

Billy points at Stan.

Billy you're looking at a man in *charge* here boys!

Joey and Harry stare at Stan.

Joey are we?

Billy let me tell ya something joey will ya please?

Joey go on

Billy in this world there's two different types of person

Joey is there?

Billy there's the type that do nothing say nothing and generally die without a whimper

Billy points at Harry.

a bit like *you* harry

Harry what *about* me?

Billy you lack motivation

Harry that's *bollocks* that is!

Billy is it?

Joey prove it

Harry clocks Joey.

Harry i don't have to it's self-evident

Joey not to me it ain't

Harry my ebullience fills the air

Joey smells the air and winces.

Joey is that what it is?

Harry alright i'll give you an example remember that time we went dancing?

Joey where?

Harry croydon

Joey you call that dancing?

Harry alright i was a bit sloshed

Joey what about it?

Harry faces Billy.

Harry we went to this club in croydon

Joey fucking dive it was

Harry the totty was top class

Joey they were all dogs

Harry anyway we musta left about . . . what?

Joey four

Harry five

Joey whatever

Harry and the taxi queue went on forever and there's no cabs

Billy not in croyden

Stan no

Harry so while this one's standing like a lemon looking at his shoes wondering what to do i nip round the corner and presto

Harry opens his arms.

i hail the only cab in the region

Billy clocks Joey.

Billy is this true?

Joey nods.

Joey it's true billy

    Billy clocks Harry and holds up his hands.

Billy alright i take it back

    Harry nods.

Harry you see

Joey so what's the other type of person?

Billy the other type?

    Joey nods.

they're a different kettle of fish completely they're like halibut to your *sole* they're the type that know what they want and go and get it and when they have it they grab it with both hands

Joey is that what *i* am then?

Billy no you're another kind

Joey you said there were only *two*?

Billy no there's two *main* ones there's loads of others they're just a bit more exclusive

    Joey grins.

Joey exclusive are they?

Billy yeh

    Joey nudges Harry.

Joey dya hear that?

Billy you know that saying 'it takes all kinds'?

Joey 'all sorts'

Billy that's it

Joey yeh

Billy points at Joey.

Billy well it does and *you're* the proof of it

Joey grins.

Joey who wants another drink?

Billy nods.

Billy we'd love another drink joey thanks

Joey walks off.

so have you seen tommy since?

Stan i have

Billy and?

Stan he's a bit peeved to say the least

Billy i bet he is

Stan he can't get his head around it

Harry around what?

Stan the fact i'm starting an enterprise

Billy points at Stan.

Billy that's cos you're an enterprising geezer

Stan is it?

Billy if he ain't the focus of attention that one he gets in a fluster and right now you're the darling of the gossip pages

Stan looks surprised.

Stan am i?

Billy nods.

why what have you heard?

Billy shakes his head.

Billy all good things stan all good things

Stan that's alright then

Billy they say that stan he's a *one* they say

Stan do they?

Billy straight up

Stan he's a one *what*?

Billy he's got *balls* they say

Stan looks down at his crotch.

Stan well of course i have

Billy i mean it takes a man of mettle to move to streatham

Stan looks perturbed.

Stan what's wrong with streatham?

Billy well it's hardly the sierra nevada is it?

Stan where's that?

Billy it's a mountain range

Stan stares at Billy.

Stan well no in that case it ain't

Billy forsaking the streets you grew up in . . . your friends and family

Billy points outside.

i mean that's *history* out there

Stan looks outside.

those are the streets you rode your first bike and kicked your first ball and stole your first ice lolly

Harry points outside.

Harry those are the *streets* stan

Stan clocks Harry.

Billy knock down ginger

Harry penny up the wall

Billy lisa behind the bikesheds

Stan chuckles.

remember?

Stan nods.

you can't put a price on that

Stan tommy had a word for it

Billy for what?

Stan 'memories of unbridled youth'

Harry looks awe-struck.

Harry that's beautiful that is

Stan he's got a way with words tommy

Billy he's got a way with *bollocks* more like i mean how can memories be unbridled that's fucking *stupid* and besides he probably nicked it

Harry from where?

Billy from i dunno a record sleeve

Harry yeh but he still memorized it

Billy anyone can memorize the hard part's thinking it up

Harry i suppose

Stan no i dunno

Billy what?

Stan i mean we all memorize things but it's *what* that's important

Harry how dya mean?

Stan well take me i store a lot up there . . .

Stan taps his temple.

but it's all trivial things like birthdays and numbers

Billy shakes his head.

Billy that ain't trivial stan

Stan ain't it?

Billy *no* . . . ! i mean say you was to forget lou's birthday

Stan heaven forbid

Billy your days'd be ended

Stan that's true

Billy points at Stan.

Billy her birthday's a lot more vital than some poxy pop lyric i tell ya

Stan i take your point

Billy it's different for tommy you see

Harry why?

Billy b/cos he's got nothing

Harry he's got *loads*!

Billy tell me what?

Harry a flash car

Billy it's only metal

Harry a nice pad

Billy it's only mortar

Harry gucci shoes

Billy they're only leather

Stan well snakeskin actually

Billy it don't *matter*!

Harry what matters billy?

Billy other *things*!

Harry like what?

Billy like things you can *touch*

Harry say one?

Billy *love* for instance

   Harry chuckles.

what's up?

   Harry shakes his head.

Harry love don't exist billy

Billy says who?

Harry tommy

Billy it don't exist for *him* perhaps that's true but it exists for others

Harry like who?

Billy like take stan you love lou don't you?

Stan i suppose

Billy she's a darling

Stan she's alright

Billy she's the woman you share your *life* with for christ sake!

Stan frowns.

Stan she has her uses

Billy stares at Stan.

Billy well i must say stan i'm dismayed i always thought you were blissfully wed

Stan me and the missus?

Billy stares at Stan.

Billy who else!?

Stan that's what she puts out

Billy you mean you're not?

Stan well you must know she *talks* to you

Billy shakes his head.

Billy she never divulges her private business stan let me *assure* you

Stan that's something

Billy she's the *soul* of discretion that one

Stan good

Billy i mean sometimes she *hints* at domestic strife but i say quite categorically you're stan's wife go lay your troubles elsewhere

Stan you what?

Billy i mean it's not that i don't have *compassion* but please there's an unspoken bond between men and i'm not gonna break it am i i mean not for some poxy

woman i don't care *how* distressed she appears or *how*
on the verge of crisis i say lou i'm sorry to do this to ya
but i'm not an agony aunt i can't burden myself with
your internal tangles i've my *own* stresses to preside over
she says billy but i need to *share* i say lou quite frankly
darling i couldn't care i mean i'm not being blunt but
you've got some front putting me in this position it's a
liberty i can't be all things to all souls at all times it's
impossible i have to draw the line she says be like that
i say i will and while you're at it don't be shrill

Billy shakes his head.

i don't like shrill women harry they annoy me

Harry nods.

Harry i agree

Billy shakes his head.

Billy she loses it when i say that stan she goes *mad* i
have to *scram* she begs me not to of course and
sometimes i must confess she can be very alluring oh yes
she can be quite a tease i don't mean to diss her but . . .

Billy taps under his eye.

i'd keep em peeled i mean i'm not saying she's *flighty*
exactly no but then again let's face it i'm not saying she's
not neither dya know what i mean?

Stan stares at Billy.

Stan i'm not sure i do no

Billy i mean weaker men might be tempted

Harry like who?

Billy well who ain't with us?

Harry how dya mean?

Billy opens his arms.

Billy among us

Stan you mean tommy?

Billy looks taken aback.

Billy that's a bit *harsh* stan

Stan what is?

Billy but now that you say it . . .

Stan i haven't

Billy you see harry?

Harry what?

Billy points at Stan.

Billy he says he don't love her but he soon gets possessive

Harry shakes his head.

Harry love ain't real it's plastic billy

Billy says who?

Harry tommy

Billy you said yourself *you* loved sally

Harry reconsiders.

Harry that's true

Billy and who can blame ya she was a *honey*

Harry she was perfect

Billy she was more than perfect stan she was flawless

Stan that's what he meant

Billy brassy blondes are two-a-penny but she had a face that *wore* i tell ya

Harry the day that lady left me billy was the day the world stopped singing my tune

Stan and Billy look taken aback.

Billy dya hear that?

Stan yeh

Billy shakes his head.

Billy it's always the quiet ones

Stan what is?

Billy that have all the raw emotion

Stan is it?

Billy they have a cartel on it or something

Harry shakes his head.

Harry i weren't quiet in *her* company billy i'd never stop gabbing i don't think i had *one* thought in all the time i saw her i didn't tell her about not *one* single thought no joke no matter *how* pointless or obscure no sooner had it entered there . . .

Harry taps his temple.

than i was saying it much to her chagrin of course she didn't know what i was on about half the time and nor did *i* to be fair i didn't have a clue not an inkling but that didn't stop me oh no that made it worse i used to look at myself and think 'harry give it a break for fuck sake will ya can't you see she's bored to tears she'll leave ya in a minute mate' but did i take heed – did i fuck – i was too busy yapping to listen i was on a roll and nothing could stop me not even the queen

Stan looks bemused.

Stan what about the queen?

Harry she coulda strolled in wherever we were and sally coulda tugged me and said 'look there's the queen in all her regalia with a fag in her hand and a brandy in the other' and i wouldn't have even jolted not a twitch i'd have carried on as normal that's how *bad* it was billy i mean i know it's hard to believe me being so *reticent* and everything . . . but in *her* presence

Harry shakes his head.

i was hopeless

Billy nods.

Billy that's *real* love that is you see

Stan how?

Billy he made a prat of himself

Harry nods.

Harry i did

Billy opens his arms.

Billy you see it *does* exist forget what tommy said he was talking to joey

Harry looks bemused.

Harry so what?

Billy he simplifies things

Harry why should he do that for joey?

Billy taps his temple.

Billy b/cos he's slow

Harry but you said he had the common touch?

Billy he has

Harry well?

Billy let me explain

Harry please do

Billy it's a curious world we belong to

Harry is it?

Billy haven't you noticed?

Harry it ain't exactly straightforward no

Billy it's straight*backward* more like

Harry straight*zigzag*

Billy straight*curvy*

Harry everything's topsy-turvy

Billy points at Harry.

Billy that's right

Harry points at Billy.

Harry i see what you mean

Billy dya see what i mean?

Harry stares at Billy.

Harry well no not really

Billy what i mean is things are seldom as they should be

Harry in what way?

Billy well say you order a pizza and ask for extra chillis and when the pizza comes not only does it not *have* extra chillis it don't have *any* chillis

Harry nods.

Harry i know that one

Billy that's what i'm chatting about

Harry i see

Stan how does this relate to joey?

Billy well the world applies strange principles

Stan such as?

Billy the simpler you are the more people like you and joey gets on with everyone

Harry so?

Billy what does that tell you about him?

Harry and Billy Stare at each other. Joey walks on with four shorts. Instead of his shirt he has on a brightly-coloured girl's crop t-shirt emblazoned with a crude banner such as 'Fuck Me' or 'I'm a Bitch'. It is far too small for him and still has its price tag.

Joey i'm not being funny . . .

Billy sighs.

Billy here we go

Joey but there i was standing at the bar minding my affair when this honey – and i mean *honey* harry – spills her drink on me

The boys look up and see the t-shirt for the first time.

all down my shirt

Billy i don't believe this

Joey soaked to the skin i was so she apologises like crazy and *i* being the gentleman i am say listen love don't worry about it it's only an 'yves saint laurent' and she *gasps* and says how can i repay ya and i say i can think

of a few things and she goes saucy and i go what can
i get ya and she goes a diet coke and i go who for and
she goes me and i go funny you don't look like you need
to diet

Joey raises his eyebrows. Harry clocks Billy.

Harry slow hey?

Joey what?

Harry go on

Joey well i'm *well* in as you can imagine we start
bubbling and next thing i know she's peeling my shirt off

Harry she isn't?

Joey she is

Harry the dirty dish

Joey so i say hold up what's going on and she's goes i'll
wash it and i go what here and she goes no silly at my
flat and i go what good's that and she goes you can pick
it up and i go when and she goes anytime you like
gorgeous

Harry she never?

Joey she did

Harry the filthy bitch

Joey and in the meantime . . .

Joey shows off the t-shirt.

she gives me this

The boys stare at the t-shirt.

what dya reckon?

Billy it's very you joey

Joey it's brand new she bought it this after

Joey inspects the price tag.

fifteen quid

Stan joey i've thought about it and the job's yours

Joey what job?

Stan at the bistro

Joey grins.

Joey is it?

Stan nods.

Stan you'll be an asset to the business

Joey i appreciate that stan you're a diamond

Joey looks at Harry and Billy.

ain't he a diamond boys?

Billy nods.

Billy the top rank

Joey points at Stan.

Joey you're the top rank

Joey raises his pint.

bottoms up

They all swig their pints.

well this calls for a bottle of bubbly

Joey clocks Billy.

a bottle of bubbly billy?

Billy nods.

Billy lovely

Joey walks off. Harry looks curious.

Harry here stan?

Stan what?

Harry what made you wanna do it?

Stan do what?

Harry open a bistro

Stan it's personal

Harry you mean you can't tell us?

Billy you can tell us anything we're your best mates

Stan it's something i was told

Harry when?

Stan when i was young

Harry what about?

Stan about rod stewart funnily enough

Harry looks surprised.

Harry rod stewart?

Stan about his upbringing in glasgow

Harry what about it?

Stan well his dad used to work in the shipyards

Harry shit

Billy talk about deprivation

Harry i know

Stan and everyday at some ungodly hour a clapped out old bus would chug down the cobbled streets picking up the workmen

Billy shakes his head.

Billy this is obscene

Harry burlesque

Billy serene

Harry grotesque

Stan anyhow during the hols his dad got him work so he'd rise at five and jump on with him

Billy *five*!?

Stan yeh

Harry is this a joke?

Stan no it's gospel

Billy flaming jocks

Stan anyway the bus weren't big enough for all the men so half of em would cling to the bars from outside

Billy sounds like the two five three

Harry yeh

Stan so one day our rod's clinging on with all his might when the bus hits a light and pulls up beside a roller

Billy a roller hey?

Harry lovely

Stan now rod's not seen a roller before

Billy not in glasgow

Harry no

Stan and his eyes light up like little sparklers and he says to his dad dad what's that and his dad says son that's a rolls royce and rod says yeh but how – what – why –

and his dad says i dunno son i dunno and rod reaches out a tiny arm and stretches as far as he can and just about gets a finger on it and he yells look dad i can touch it and his dad scowls and says yeh you can touch it son but believe me . . .

Stan shakes his head.

you can *never* touch it

Harry miserable sod

Billy i hope he dies of cancer

Stan raises his hand.

Stan but hold on there's an epitaph

Billy looks impressed.

Billy oh there's an 'epitaph' is there?

Billy clocks Harry.

i didn't realise

Stan years later when he's living in london he has his first number one and visits his dad

Harry that's nice

Billy yes i do like that

Stan so he strolls up to the same old house in the same old street and knocks on the door

Harry and Billy nod.

Harry and?

Billy what happened?

Stan his dad answers it

Harry what does he say?

Stan shakes his head.

Stan nothing

Harry looks bemused.

Harry what?

Stan he's speechless

Harry why?

Stan b/cos standing there in front of his face is a spanking new shiny silver shadow

Harry looks stunned.

Harry no?

Stan nods.

Stan straight up

Harry now there's a touch

Stan and rod takes the old man's hand and walks him to the car and says look dad . . .

Stan knocks on the table.

you can touch it

Harry looks stunned.

Harry he said that?

Stan yeh

Harry shakes his head.

Harry well would you credit it?

Stan and he pulls out the key and plops it in his dad's pyjama pocket

Harry you mean he was wearing pyjamas?

Stan well i dunno he mighta been

Harry why was it a sunday or something?

Stan i'm just *elaborating* to the story

Harry well that's a mighty fine story stan

Stan thanks

Harry i've always liked rod stewart

Stan you never said?

Harry well i couldn't admit it but now . . .

Harry opens his arms.

well i feel liberated

Billy i tell ya that's the kinda son i want

Harry a rock star?

Billy no one with manners

Harry oh

Billy he'll leave home when he's good and able

Harry when's that?

Billy fifteen max

Harry okay

Billy and he'll come back when he's got me a motor

Harry then what?

Billy then he can fuck off!

Stan what have you ever got *your* dad?

Billy checks.

Billy you what?

126

Stan you heard

Billy i'll tell you about my dad shall i?

Stan go on

Billy he'd knock me down with a feather cradle me in his arms read me the riot act tell me not to slack kick the shit out of me give me a smack tell me how to talk to ladies – lovely – look after mum – say what's for dinner eat it all up and meanwhile . . .

Billy points at Stan.

stay the right side of the *law* my son don't court trouble or you'll be hung your remains'll be strewn across the tarmac

Stan they put him away didn't they?

Billy best place for him the nut

Harry it's a shame about that

Billy what is?

Harry madness running in the family

Billy it skips a generation though

Harry does it?

Billy can't you tell?

Billy opens his arms.

i'm as sane as a baby octopus

Harry and Stan stare at Billy. Joey staggers on. Beaten black and blue. T-shirt torn. Hair torn. Cuts and bruises. Bandages. He shakes his head.

Joey okay this you are *not* gonna believe . . .

The boys turn and stare at Joey.

Harry what the fuck . . . !?

Joey opens his arms.

Joey i only asked for some bubbly

Harry where?

Joey at the bar

Harry with who?

Joey linda

The boys stare at Joey.

Harry your baby?

Joey she went completely crazy!

Harry why!?

Joey she saw the t-shirt

Harry twigs.

Harry oh shit

Joey she asked where i got it

Harry what did you say?

Joey what could i say i couldn't tell her the truth could i?

Harry no

Joey she'd have gone nuts

The boys stare at Joey, beaten black and blue.

Harry so what dya make up?

Joey i told her they were the height of fashion i said *all* the boys are wearing em in town

Harry and?

Joey shakes his head.

Joey she didn't buy it

Harry so she went for you?

Joey well no first she gave me another chance she's not unreasonable harry

Harry no of course

Joey points at Harry.

Joey she said the truth this time joey nothing but i'm warning you

Joey shakes his head.

she was dead serious

Harry so you conceded?

Joey no i told her another lie

Harry which?

Joey i said i had a twin sister and it was our birthday . . .

Billy points at Joey.

Billy hence the bubbly?

Joey points at Billy.

Joey exactly

Billy nods.

Billy good thinking joey

Joey and this was her present and i was just trying out the size

Joey taps his temple.

quick see

Harry how did she twig?

Joey she asked my star sign

Harry what did you say?

Joey aries

Billy in *winter*?

Joey opens his arms.

Joey how could *i* know?

Stan shakes his head.

Stan oh joey

Joey shakes his head.

Joey it wasn't pretty

Harry i bet

Joey raises his hand.

Joey but wait it gets worse

Harry how?

Joey she cancelled our date

Harry no?

Joey straight up

Harry the hard-nosed tart

Joey it's okay i found a replacement

Harry so fast?

Joey i couldn't help it there were women *swarming* over me!

Harry how come?

Joey they were trying to nurse me i swear if you ever want female attention get on the wrong end of a beating boys it works *wonders*

Joey raises his eyebrows.

i'm not kidding

Harry shakes his head.

Harry you get all the luck you know that?

Joey nods.

Joey i went over and thanked linda personally

Harry how did she take it?

Joey she threw the till at me

Harry no?

Stan well she's a big girl

Joey i did quite well out of it as it goes

Harry how?

Joey it broke open

Joey dips his hands in his pockets.

look

Joey pulls out a sea of loose change and lets it spill through his fingers. He grins.

loads of readies!

The boys stare at all the change. There's a lot of it.

Billy joey seeing as you're so flush . . .

Joey yeh?

Billy you can put some in the jukebox

Joey nods.

Joey fine

Billy rod stewart perhaps

Joey love to

Billy clocks Stan.

Billy which one was it?

Stan what?

Billy his first number one

Stan looks taken aback.

Harry maggie may

Stan you're a bit au fait?

Harry well he's my specialised subject

Billy clocks Joey

Billy put on maggie may

Joey walks off.

i tell ya there's two kinds of people what like rod stewart

Stan clocks Harry.

Stan two is there?

Billy that's right stan . . . there's the people at the top and the people at the bottom

Harry looks bemused.

Harry i'm not with ya?

Billy he's one of them phenomenons only the *extremes* of society can appreciate harry

Harry like who?

Billy like the old dears in palmers green who can't get enough of the fella

Harry nods.

Harry it's his lucid charm

Billy and then there's the cream

Harry the cream?

Billy points at Harry.

Billy people like *you* harry . . . people with zest and all round pazazz

Harry you mean snazz?

Billy i mean razamatazz

Stan i thought he lacked motivation?

Billy no that's joey

Stan you said it was *him*

Billy that's before he said about croydon . . . the cab queue remember . . . ? i tell ya that really impressed me that did

Stan why?

Billy Well many's the time i've been stumped for transport on a saturday night without a shining light for guidance

Harry that's right

Billy points at Harry.

Billy but *you* harry you took the bull by the horns and got on your high horse and paid a pony for a donkey ride

Harry nods.

Harry thank you

Billy meanwhile what was joey doing?

Harry gazing at his shoes

Billy wondering what to do

Harry poncing about like a lemon

Billy points at Stan.

Billy *you* said it

Billy clocks Stan and points at Harry.

i tell ya he's the one you want working for ya

Stan stares at Harry.

Stan harry?

Billy his sheer presence will *galvanise* people

Stan looks bemused.

Stan are you sure?

Billy don't knock it stan

Stan i'm not knocking anything i love Harry but . . .

Billy what?

Stan i've never seen him like that

Billy you know your trouble?

Stan what's that?

Billy you're prejudiced

Harry no it's just the light

Billy You're like the guy on top of the hill . . .

Harry charlie big potatoes

Billy that's it . . . looking down on his flock . . . sneering

Stan me?

Billy i mean now you're an entrepreneur

Stan smirks.

Stan come off it

Billy forgotten your friends have we?

Billy and Stan stare at each other.

Harry what is it then?

Stan stares at Harry.

Stan i wanna *make* something of myself is something wrong in that?

Harry you're fine as you are

Stan shakes his head.

Stan not to me

Harry frowns.

Harry you have faults admittedly

Stan none of my family ever stood up harry

Harry you what?

Stan they took their lot with a smile and good grace and made do

Stan nods.

sure

Stan shakes his head.

but they never took a chance

Billy you had a good home

Stan i don't deny it

Billy you never shook with fear as you climbed the steps and pressed the bell and prayed to god your mum would answer it

Billy points at Stan.

cause to be thankful stan

Stan and i am

Billy good

Stan they're diamond people my folks i know that . . . but . . . they settled for nothing . . . scrimping . . . saving . . . lining someone else's pocket . . . they had no sense of what they wanted . . . what they could enjoy . . . they never showed me the world and said 'look there's the world stan go and kick arse young man it's there for the taking . . . all of it'

Stan shakes his head.

never

Stan opens his arms.

and look at me . . . i'm pushing thirty and i'm just the same . . . doing the same thing . . . the same mistakes . . . in twenty years i'll still be here in this same pub only on *their* side of the bar and they'll be *dead* . . . and i'll be drinking to their memory . . . saying what diamond people they were . . . and everyone'll raise a glass and carry on

Stan nods.

and that's the life is it . . . ? that's what my grandad fought. for . . . ? so i can be a cunt forever . . . ? well i've tried it and i want changes . . . i've *dreams* harry

Harry i understand all that stan

   Harry raises his pint.

but taste the ale

   Harry smells the air.

smell the air

   Billy and Stan smell the air and wince.

Billy that's your ebullience again that is

   Harry opens his arms.

Harry *this* is the stuff of dreams

   Stan shakes his head.

Stan it's not so simple

Billy why not?

Stan lou's set her heart on leaving

Billy why?

Stan i dunno but something's troubling her

Billy what?

Stan something serious i reckon

Billy it's the time of the month

Stan no it ain't that she's acting up

Billy how?

Stan well when my nan died she was *glad* if anything

Billy what?

Stan on account of the flat . . . i said i'd rather *rent* the flat and live elsewhere i don't wanna live there

Billy no

Harry in your nan's flat

Stan it's not that it's streatham

Harry what?

Stan cringes.

Stan horrible place

Billy so what's the problem?

Stan she's in a *rush* . . . she wants to move *now*

Stan shakes his head.

there's no talking to her

Joey walks on. Sits down. Sups his pint. Eventually he notices all the boys are staring at him. He stares back at them.

Joey what?

The boys stare at Joey.

Billy what happened?

Joey what dya mean?

Billy well where have you *been*?

Joey at the jukebox like you said

Billy is that it?

Joey yeh

Billy so what took you?

Joey stares at Billy.

Joey i went to the kazi is that okay!?

Billy and?

Joey stands and starts to undo his flies.

Joey i got my winkle out and had a pee dya want me to show you?

The boys raise their hands together.

Harry and **Billy** and **Stan** no you're alright

Joey stares at the boys. He does up his flies. Sits down. Shakes his head.

Joey you boys are weird

Billy nods.

Billy so you put on the song then?

Joey yeh

Billy maggie may?

Joey no another one

Billy what?

Joey still rod stewart mind

Billy do you ignore tommy in the same way?

Joey what?

Billy well?

Joey tommy lets *me* pick

Billy does he?

Joey he likes my taste

Billy likes you period

Joey nods.

Joey i'd say

Billy that's why he flees when you're in need

Joey what?

Billy when you fell in the lake . . .

Harry shakes his head.

Harry oh not this again

Billy where was he your wonderful friend?

Joey i dunno

Billy *gone* . . . ! that's where . . . ! you were flapping and wailing like a *cunt* and he was nowhere near

Billy and Joey stare at each other.

or don't you remember?

Joey i remember one thing billy

Billy what's that?

Joey i didn't fall

Billy what?

Joey i was pushed

Stan says who?

Joey i do stan

Billy his mind's playing tricks

Joey no it ain't i remember it clearly . . . like it was yesterday . . . i still have nightmares

Stan do you?

Joey nods.

Joey now and then

Stan that's very enlightening

Billy why?

Stan well i never saw you as the selfless type billy

Billy nods.

Billy oh that's nice innit i only risk my neck to save my mate

Stan you did

Billy *thank* you

Stan the question is *why*

Stan and Joey stare at Billy. 'I Don't Want to Talk About It' by Rod Stewart comes on.

Harry will you listen to that

The boys fall silent. Lights fade down. Spotlight on Harry who listens intently. The lyrics strike a chord with him. Lights come up as song fades down. Harry shakes his head.

pure class

Billy nods.

Billy a blinding choice joey

Joey stan tell him your story will ya?

Harry what story?

Joey about the pyjamas

Harry you mean he *was* wearing pyjamas?

Joey stares at Harry.

Joey yeh course

Harry points at Stan.

Harry there you see i knew it

Joey so you told em?

Stan nods.

when?

Harry just now

Joey shakes his head.

Joey it's a diamond story that

Harry clocks Stan.

Harry where dya hear it?

Joey you mean you don't know?

Harry no

Joey you didn't say?

Stan shakes his head.

why not?

Stan shrugs.

Stan i didn't think it important

Joey not important it's the most important bit!

Harry what is?

Joey can i tell him?

Stan if you like

Harry tell me what?

Joey stares at Harry. Composes himself.

Joey his *dad* told him that story

Harry stares at Joey.

Harry so what?

Joey smirks.

Joey nah you don't get it his *dad* told him it

Harry stares at Joey.

Harry and?

Joey stares at Harry.

Joey think of that story a minute will ya

Harry yeh?

Joey the roller and everything we *are* talking about the same story . . . ?

Harry yeh

Joey what's it about?

Harry shrugs.

Harry You tell me

Joey i *will* tell you it's about a dad who's a cunt stifling his son and his son showing him where to *shove* it

Harry so?

Joey so his *dad* told him it

Harry and Stan stare at Joey. Billy shakes his head.

Billy listen joey stories get passed down they do the rounds they get distorted *you* of all people know that

Joey raises his eyebrows.

Joey oh do i?

Billy who says em's of no concern it's what they *tell* us that's important

Joey and what does that story tell you?

Billy it tells me our rod's a top bloke

Harry damn right!

Billy it's not all pop stars remember their folks you know

Harry no

Billy i mean i heard . . .

Billy beckons the boys closer. He lowers his voice.

i heard david bowie skipped his mum's funeral

The boys looked shocked.

Harry no?

Billy nods.

Billy straight up

Harry the little cunt

Billy he was too busy doing god knows what

Harry cascading in frocks

Billy that's right

Harry the ungrateful sod

Billy he didn't even send flowers

Harry shakes his head.

Harry and to think

Billy what?

Harry i bought his last record

Billy point at Stan.

Billy that's what happens when you make it big stan you should take heed

Billy and Stan stare at each other.

i mean take tommy

Stan what about him?

Billy he couldn't give a flying fuck about us

Stan that ain't true

Billy of *course* it is

Harry you've changed your tune haven't you?

Stan what?

Harry i thought he was banned from your do?

Stan shakes his head.

Stan not any more

Billy looks perturbed.

Billy how come?

Stan frowns.

Stan louise changed her mind

Billy why?

Stan they had words

Harry that tommy

Harry shakes his head.

he could charm a cat out of a sewer that man

Billy that's all very well but i don't have to let him in though do i?

Harry how dya mean?

Billy well it's still at mine and i'm master of my own domain

Stan it's not so simple i'm afraid

Billy why not?

Stan there's been changes

Billy what changes?

145

Stan i dunno quite how to say this billy

Billy say what?

Stan the do's at tommy's and you're not coming

Billy looks stunned.

Billy do what?

Stan shrugs.

Stan it's what louise wants

Billy how come?

Stan she won't say

Billy well I'm gonna get to the bottom of this

Billy pulls out his mobile.

Stan she ain't in

Harry where is she?

Stan at the doctor's

Harry why what's up?

Stan women's things

Billy well you tell her . . .

Billy nods.

this is tommy's doing this is

Billy points at Stan.

you tell her i'll be round . . . and i'll want explaining

The boys sup their pints. Not a whisky has been touched.

SCENE TWO

North London flat. Ironing piled up to the ceiling.
Louise is standing behind the ironing board draping a
towel around her head. Dressing gown. Billy stands
inside the doorway. Overcoat done up. Leather gloves.
He is holding a slim elegant tailor's box.

Louise you're becoming quite a fixture billy

Billy oh i can't stop lou though nothing'd thrill me more

Louise i'm sure

Billy but i'm pressed

Louise shame

Billy people to see deals to rearrange

Louise as ever

Billy we can't afford to stand idle

Louise so what warrants this fleeting call?

Billy holds out the box.

Billy i just wanted to give you this

Louise what is it?

Billy a gift

Louise for what?

Billy for wearing to the do

Louise shakes her head.

Louise i can't take it

Billy come now you've not said no before

Louise i have something

Billy but not like *this* lou

Louise even so

Billy it's of the finest cloth

Louise i know

Billy the surest stitch

Louise and that's it?

Billy what?

Louise then you'll go?

Billy raises his eyebrows.

Billy you not glad to see me i *am* surprised

Louise it's a bad time that's all

Billy holds out the box.

Billy you can try it on first lou let me look i mean it might be the wrong *size*

Louise it's fine

Billy how dya know?

Louise you've bought me loads of clothes

Billy but do they fit?

Louise snugly

Billy i wouldn't know

Louise trust me

Billy i don't see you in em do i you always dress down

Louise i don them sometimes

Billy when?

Louise special occasions

Billy holds out the box.

Billy well then this is *perfect* the very *thing* try it see if i'm wrong

Louise later

Billy why not now for heaven sake?

Louise stan's back soon

Billy nods.

Billy right

Louise and he'll want his dinner and if i ain't finished my pressing . . .

Billy whatever it is lou it smells good

Billy rubs his tummy.

it's making me quite peckish

Louise i've only two plates in the oven

Billy i understand

Louise you shoulda rung

Billy you getting in some practice?

Louise for what?

Billy the business

Louise nods.

Louise something like that yeh

Billy well on this showing i reckon they'll come flocking

Louise thanks

Billy no i mean it

Louise so was there more or can i carry on?

Billy raises his eyebrows.

Billy you're being rather short despite your haste

Louise i've explained

Billy opens his arms.

Billy no drink nothing?

Louise you're not stopping

Billy nods.

Billy i could wait for stan yeh

Billy steps inside the room. He puts the box down on the sofa.

clear the air

Billy starts undoing his coat. Same colour suit as previous scene.

it might be for the best

Louise but you're pressed?

Billy but he's back soon you said

Billy drapes his coat over the back of the sofa. He walks over to the drinks and pours himself a scotch. Louise watches him.

back from a hard day's toil

Louise starts ironing.

slaving at the furnace

Louise is silent.

sweating at the brow

Louise he works in an office

Billy all the same it can't be pleasant

Louise yeh well he'll be his own boss soon

Billy you both will

Louise i can't wait

Billy how will it feel?

Louise i dunno

Billy great

Billy points at Louise.

that's what . . . it'll feel great lou

Louise puts down the iron.

Louise it ain't easy running a bistro billy statistics prove
it

Billy so they do

Louise it's a big risk

Billy the world is rife

Louise if it goes wrong we're up the cranny

Billy it won't be funny

Louise we'll lose all our money

Billy not to mention your sense of pride

Louise nods.

Louise and you'd *know* would you?

Billy oh i'll admit i know nothing of *owning* a place lou
but it's a wish i've always harboured

Billy points at Louise.

secretly mind i'm not one to call from barges . . . screaming my most innermost dreams to all and sundry . . .
no . . . i'm more discreet

Louise or unfulfilled

Billy how dya mean?

Louise well when someone has something you don't you want it

Billy stares at Louise and nods.

Billy that's very pertinent lou

Louise just observing

Billy no coming from someone like you

Louise like what?

Billy that *knows* me a little

Billy nods.

that's very pertinent

Louise continues ironing.

i mean i like to think i'm a bit of an *enigma* you know a source of fascination to those that know me but you lou have crushed that little indulgence forever and i'm not bitter no i'm grateful . . . i mean think how long i coulda swanned around deluding myself . . . how much longer . . . it's bananas . . . snubbing invites turning down approaches and all for being enigmatic

Billy opens his arms.

which i patently ain't

Billy points at Louise.

you see that's what comes of getting to *know* someone . . . sensibly i mean slowly and over time . . . you spot things about em little slights in their character that might otherwise go untraced . . . that's the benefit . . . you're wrong of course

Louise am i?

Billy nods.

Billy oh yeh . . . blatently . . . i'm more than happy
in myself lou always have been and who can blame
me . . . ? no when i said i wanted a place i weren't
referring to a *bistro*

Louise oh

Billy no . . . though billy's bistro does have a certain
ring i admit . . . no i was thinking more of a *drinking*
den

Louise that figures

Billy billy's bar even . . . for members . . . top quality
spirits . . . imported . . . a place of solace for the refined
gent

Louise i get the picture

Billy a games room a back room a smoke room a front
room all the rooms you ever wanted and on occasion i'd
stop by . . . yeh . . . show my face . . . grace the place
with my presence . . . solve any altercation . . . treat
myself to a tipple maybe . . . look around

Billy raises his hand.

savour the moment lou

Louise that's what i'm looking forward to

Billy what is?

Louise puts down the iron.

Louise being in charge

Billy points at Louise.

Billy you said that 'eloquently'

Louise saying you can have that table or that table but not that one it's reserved

Billy a lovely feeling

Louise turning away the riff-raff

Billy of course

Louise changing the menu

Billy the cook

Louise the staff

Billy telling em their time's up

Louise writing em a reference

Billy oh yeh

Billy nods.

very rewarding

Louise and talking to the punters billy

Billy looks bemused.

Billy talking to em?

Louise yeh

Billy shakes his head.

Billy nah you don't wanna do that

Louise but i *do* that's what i want *most*

Billy nah

Billy shakes his head.

sorry

Louise aah you got no idea

Billy what?

Louise you'll close down in six months

Billy i ain't even opened yet!

Louise you gotta use your *nous* billy if you want em back . . . show em you value them . . . sit down . . . get em a drink on the house

Billy points at Louise.

Billy you'll be good at this lark

Louise they'll say lou you look well i'll say i've been away they'll say where i'll say spain they'll say we've missed you around here we really have you light up the place i'll feign modesty . . . it'll be just as i always wanted billy . . . everything i dreamed

Billy you'll be a queen

Louise quite so

Billy then again a palate for power ain't always looked on kindly . . . no . . . take tommy

Louise sighs.

Louise oh don't start billy

Billy no go on

They stare at each other.

Louise what about him?

Billy everyone's angel he ain't

Louise he has mates

Billy but do they like him?

Louise they *abide* by him

Billy but is it the same thing?

Louise that bloke has more messages on his voicemail than he knows what to do with . . . i get quite jealous

Billy shakes his head.

Billy not an admirable trait louise

Louise they ring from all over . . . at all times . . . people he hardly knows they know of *him* they get his number they make a call and he accomodates . . . that's tommy

Billy always certain

Louise at least in public

Billy what dya mean?

Louise points at Billy.

Louise there's an enigma billy . . . if you want a model

Billy i don't

Louise but beneath the surface . . .

Billy frowns.

Billy is he happy lou?

Louise he struggles like the rest of us

Billy more so

Louise probably . . . poor thing

Billy sneers at Louise.

Billy do me a favour

Louise what?

Billy tommy!?

Louise and why not?

Billy mister snakeskin shoes!?

Louise raises her eyebrows.

Louise oh really?

Billy he ain't struggled in his *life* that one and why should he!?

Louise you've changed your tune

Billy it's *me* you wanna watch out for lou if anyone

Louise you!?

Billy opens his arms.

Billy well have a look!

Louise what?

Billy opens his arms further.

Billy here i stand

Louise yeh?

Billy opens his arms further.

Billy right before ya for fuck sake

Louise and?

Billy frowns.

Billy uniquely troubled

Louise scoffs.

Louise and what troubles ya?

Billy all sorts you've no idea

Louise then help me

Billy well this nation for starters

Louise what?

Billy it's fucked!

Louise why?

Billy cos no-one watched *out* for it that's why i dunno the rain came down and no-one put up the awnings they just let it wash away

Billy walks over to the window and peers out.

now look

Billy sneers at what he sees.

it's all turned to rust

Louise stares at Billy.

Louise you know billy you confuse me before you said . . .

Billy that was in the *past* lou

Louise what changed?

Billy i dunno nothing that ain't the point

Louise he's always been a bone with you

Billy and you never argued . . . in fact that's what bonded us . . . i thought . . . a mutual loathing

Louise is silent.

or was it the money?

Louise stares at Billy.

Louise i never asked for anything billy let's get this straight shall we?

Billy you took it though

Louise if you wanna give handouts that's up to you

Billy and i *do* lou i love giving ya it makes my day

Louise fine then i'll have it

Billy you not proud?

Louise i wanna get away

Billy do you now?

Louise and every bit counts

Billy why so keen?

Louise what dya mean?

Billy what coulda happened?

Louise who said it did?

Billy you wanna see him in a good light all of a sudden

Billy frowns.

i just thought

Louise let's drop the subject hey i don't wanna talk
about tommy i've *told* you

Billy you've an impaired image of him lou and i dunno
why

Louise right that's it

Billy turns to face Louise.

Billy what?

Louise you're starting to annoy me

Billy opens his arms.

Billy i thought i was being cordial

Louise i've things to *do* billy not least make the gravy –
lay the table – change . . .

Billy the table hey?

Louise yeh

Billy you not eating with the telly?

Louise not tonight no

Billy why?

Louise i wanted something different

Billy nods.

Billy does stan know?

Louise no

Billy well i hope he can make it

Louise what?

Billy a whole dinner at the table . . . that's not like the stan you've described

Louise he'll be fine

Billy perhaps you should line up some afters i mean he might need an incentive

Billy raises his eyebrows.

if you know what i mean?

Louise glares at Billy.

Louise our conversation will suffice thank you billy

Billy of course it will i'm being unkind . . . no you've a lot to talk about you two ain't ya . . . ? it being a state of flux . . . and that

Billy nods.

a *lot* to talk about

Louise we always have

Billy *now* who's changing their tune?

Louise i've just come to my senses that's all

Billy how?

Louise well it was always doomed wasn't it?

Billy what was?

Louise our friendship

Billy why?

Louise b/cos you're stan's *mate*

　Billy raises his eyebrows.

Billy oh so i'm still his *mate* now am i that's a turn up

　Louise nods.

Louise you're taking this too personally you know that

Billy what?

Louise whatever's on your mind

Billy which is?

Louise i dunno do i and now i'm short of time

　Billy nods.

Billy so that's the end of us then is it?

　Louise points at Billy.

Louise i tell ya what i've had an idea why don't you press on and i'll give you a buzz . . . say . . . tuesday . . . whenever . . . we'll get together . . . talk this through . . . it'll be fine

Billy no charge?

Louise not this time no

　Billy looks impressed.

Billy your company for *free* how about that?

Louise a token of my esteem

Billy for me?

Louise yeh

Billy but we're doomed?

Louise let's see hey

Billy but you're stan's *wife* for christ sake what's the flaming world coming to!?

Louise we'll reset the rules

Billy in what way?

Louise leave out the personal stuff . . . perhaps

Billy but i like that *best* lou . . . all those things of you . . . and your marriage

Billy nods.

very much

Billy pours himself a refill. Louise watches him. She shakes her head.

Louise it ain't fair billy

Billy on who?

Louise my husband

Billy he can't hear

Louise still

Billy i like to lend an ear lou

Louise and i *too* but it can't go on can't you see that?

Billy no

Louise i'm *moving* billy

Billy opens his arms.

Billy i *know* that lou you told me *first* remember back when we was pals all those moons ago it was *me* what told the boys what defended you from all the abuse

Louise what abuse?

Billy vitriolic it was

Louise what for?

Billy for taking our stan of course

Louise gapes at Billy.

Louise *i* never took him anything he took *me* he saw me and that was it he was gone i have that affect on men i dunno why

Billy you don't entice it?

Louise frowns.

Louise i don't try

Billy you're a natural

Louise i was content before all this a real livewire i was i'd prance about with the best of em

Billy a bit like stan

Louise now look at me

Billy raises his eyebrows.

Billy not impressed?

Louise that's why i'm starting afresh

Billy you're opening a bistro lou don't get carried away it's hardly ground-breaking

Louise well it is for *me* . . . for *us* . . . and i'm sorry if that doesn't suit you billy . . . but that's what it is

They stare at each other. Louise continues ironing.

Billy nods.

Billy i see

Louise i hope so

Billy i don't have a lot of folk to talk to that's the problem

Louise is silent.

there's you

Louise is silent.

and then that's it

Louise is silent.

strange don't ya think?

Louise is silent.

i thought you'd be an ally

Louise well you was wrong

Billy evidently

Louise and i can't change my mind

Billy i wouldn't have the temerity

Louise fine

Billy after all you know what they say?

Louise looks up at Billy.

Louise no what's that?

Billy they say you're a strong-willed lady

Louise do they?

Billy certainly

Louise who does?

Billy everyone

Louise is that so

Billy of *course* it is . . . they say you're an *ox*

Louise and what does *that* mean?

Billy it means you're a *lion*

Louise a lion?

Billy yep

Louise i'm not sure i like that

Billy yes you do lion's are god's chosen creatures lou they've got big . . .

> *Louise glares at Billy.*

Louise what?

Billy *manes*

Louise oh

Billy they're fearsome beasts

> *Louise glares at Billy.*

Louise are you alluding to me?

Billy i'm alluding to your fearsome *spirit* . . . your indomitable *force*

> *Billy points at Louise.*

whatever knocks this shoddy world may throw at ya lou you ride em with the cocky cavalier courage of a carthorse

> *Louise stares at Billy.*

Louise and what knocks are these?

Billy i'm supposing

Louise i've had none

Billy you displeased?

Louise should i be?

Billy a seamless road isn't lined with thrills louise one might take a detour

Louise well not me

Billy so you're alright i take it?

Louise i'm fine

Billy holds up his hands.

Billy i'm just checking

Louise what have you heard billy?

Billy nothing

Louise it's all lies

Billy smirks to himself.

Billy i've not heard nothing

Louise i know how you boys talk

Billy not about *you* lou

Louise are you sure?

Billy nods.

Billy tommy been playing games has he there's a thing

Louise the do's at *his* billy and that's that i can't be switching like the wind

Billy one thing lou

Louise what?

Billy why?

Louise b/cos it's him

They stare at each other.

satisfied?

Billy opens his arms.

Billy is that it?

Louise he and stan have a bond you know that

Billy they hardly see each other!

Louise they go back

Billy and i don't?

Louise it's better this way

Billy and i'm barred can you explain?

Louise i want no scenes

Billy what dya mean?

Louise i want an amicable evening is that so much?

Billy opens his arms.

Billy you know *me* lou i never misbehave

Louise i wanna look back and say that was a top do

Billy you will

Louise i've been to a few but that was the pick of the crop

Billy it was

Louise we did the lambada the foxtrot the pina colada we drank champagne and everyone enjoyed themselves make no mistake

Billy points at Louise.

Billy and you looked gorgeous in that dress

They stare at each other. Louise shakes her head.

Louise i'm not wearing it billy

Billy opens his arms.

Billy oh come on lou what harm is there?

Louise i've told you

Billy you've not even opened it open it and then see

Louise i've got something

Billy and is it nice?

Louise nods.

Louise presentable

Billy i'm sorry i'll miss it

Louise stares at Billy. She continues ironing.

Louise yeh well

Billy raises his hand.

Billy oh don't feel bad lou i wouldn't go anyway

Louise looks up at Billy.

Louise and why not?

Billy i'd look a fool!

Louise you could buy a new suit

Billy i'm not referring to my dress sense lou

Louise oh

Billy no

Billy looks indignant.

please

Billy holds out his sleeves.

this is top quality garb

Billy strokes the fabric.

handmade

Louise what then?

Billy i'd be turning up at the do i arranged . . . with all the accoutrements . . . i even hired the kareoke

Louise you never?

Billy i flaming did . . . you're damn right . . . it was gonna be a right proper send-off . . . now it's all gone to waste

Billy pours himself a refill. Louise watches him.

Louise why's everyone so rueful i dunno

Billy who?

Louise well there's you

Billy and with good reason i'm a man defeated ain't i?

Louise says who?

Billy it's obvious!

Billy opens his arms.

tommy has the do your adoration stan's compliance and what do *i* hey?

Louise he's none too chipper neither if you must know

Billy raises his eyebrows.

Billy why what's up?

Louise oh i dunno he's upset he missed a horse race

Billy looks puzzled.

Billy tommy don't like racing?

Louise oh no?

Billy that's not like him i wonder what he's up to?

Louise it's only stan has any good to say

Billy and you know why don't you?

Louise looks at Billy inquiringly.

oh come on lou

Billy taps his temple.

think about it

Louise frowns.

cos he's got you

Louise smirks.

Louise fuck off

Billy it's *true*!

Billy peers at Louise up and down and nods.

i could come home to that quite readily

Louise glares at Billy.

Louise shut up billy

Billy chuckles into his glass.

i'm warning you this is stan's flat and while you're here you'll show him respect

Billy of *course* i respect stan lou . . .

Louise well

Billy he's a man on the *move* that one . . . i mean i can say that now he ain't here . . . we don't want *him*

hearing it it might go to his head and then we'd all be on the kicking end wouldn't we especially you . . . you being his wife . . . and that . . . you see him more than we do . . . it's only natural . . . but as he's not . . . and we are . . . so to speak

Billy nods.

i can tell you i've always had a grudging awe for him

Billy raises his hand.

no don't laugh

Louise i wasn't going to

Billy i mean i know some see him different

Louise who?

Billy well let's not get into betrayals here

Louise no honestly billy i'd like to know how he's thought of

Billy by who?

Louise the boys

Billy why?

Louise well he'd not been rung in ages before this latest news

Billy of you leaving?

Louise what else?

Billy shakes his head.

Billy and they was devastated when i told em lou

Louise was they?

Billy gasps.

Billy oh inconsolable they was

Louise really?

Billy a hush descended em . . . all the way to tooting it went

Louise i thought they was vitriolic?

Billy after that i mean

Louise i see

Billy quiet as doormouses they fell especially harry

Louise ahh bless

Billy well you know what he's like

Louise and what about tommy?

Billy tommy?

Louise joey i mean

Billy joey was . . .

Louise and tommy?

  Billy opens his arms.

Billy *now* who's bringing him up?

Louise i wanna know what he *said* that's all!

Billy *nothing* i told ya!

Louise he musta!

  Billy frowns.

Billy hardly . . . he was strangely unchanged . . . said he'd seen it coming

  Louise looks perturbed.

Louise had he?

Billy *liked* the idea

Louise did he?

Billy you were in a rut and best shot he said

Louise the cheeky swine!

Billy you said the same!

Louise i can say what i *like* about me that's different

  They fall silent.

Billy fine

Louise tell me something billy?

  Billy looks at Louise inquiringly.

dya think i'm dull?

  Billy stares at Louise and her ironing.

be honest

  Billy nods.

Billy tommy said did he?

  Louise is silent.

and that matters?

  Louise is silent. Billy points at her.

he's an image of you lou but he's only denying himself

Louise of what?

Billy of what he's missing out on

Louise which is?

Billy domestic bliss

  Billy opens his arms.

i mean look at this

Billy looks around the room.

your darling abode

Louise don't be kind billy we're moving out

Billy and i'm sure streatham is very nice

Louise it is

Billy but this is more than pleasant . . . i mean take a look

Billy holds out his arm.

flowers in the corner . . . ming vase

Louise it's a copy

Billy all the same stan's a very lucky fella you know that i mean call it dull if you will but this is man's eternal wish

Louise what is?

Billy i don't care *how* complex a bloke is all he craves is simple things

Billy pours himself a refill. Louise watches him.

are you gonna have kids?

Louise looks surprised.

Louise you what?

Billy soon

Louise nods.

Louise perhaps

Billy oh stan'll love that

Louise dya reckon?

Billy oh yeh he'll be made *up*!

Billy opens his arms.

just think . . . tiny little tots tittering about . . . ? lovely

They stare at each other. Billy looks towards the door.

where is he anyway the crafty sod?

Louise i'll tell him you called shall i?

Billy turns to face Louise.

Billy what?

Louise if you've gotta dash

They stare at each other. Louise frowns.

nah he'll be well cut up

Louise continues ironing.

no it'd be a shame if you came round and didn't wait for stan

Billy walks over to the sofa.

don't ya think?

Billy sits.

he'd say what he came all this way and didn't wait for me the cunt?

Louise shakes her head.

what a cunt

Billy picks up the remote control and flicks on the TV.

he'd be heart-broken

Billy pulls out his cigarettes.

Billy and at the end of the day lou he'd be right

Louise he's your mate

Billy you're only his wife

Louise for goodness sake

Billy i mean don't get me wrong i've enjoyed our time together i really have it's been a while since i've spent time with a woman and you lou are a bastion of your gender let me tell ya i mean i've known some over the years you've probably heard you wouldn't wanna be seen *dead* with let alone in public places where someone might see ya they may hold it against ya especially in broad daylight dya know what i mean?

   Louise puts down the iron.

Louise are you getting at something billy?

Billy fag?

Louise no thanks

Billy you cutting down?

Louise i've given up

   Billy looks impressed.

Billy since when?

Louise yesterday

Billy that's impressive

Louise it's no big thing

Billy no i never knew you was so disciplined?

Louise i'm strong-willed remember?

   Billy smiles and nods.

Billy oh yeh

Louise an ox you said

Billy lights up. He nods.

Billy a stunning ox at that

> *Louise glares at Billy. She tuts and continues ironing.*
> *He gazes at the TV a while.*

so you and tommy go back is it?

> *Billy nods.*

that's nice

> *Long pause.*

Louise not me and tommy *stan* and tommy

> *Billy nods.*

Billy oh yeh

> *Long pause.*

you have a bond?

> *Long pause.*

Louise *they* do yeh

> *Billy nods. Long pause.*

Billy you know him well?

Louise *i'd* say so

Billy perhaps that's the trouble

Louise hey?

Billy perhaps you know him *too* well

Louise i'm not with ya

> *Billy nods.*

Billy i think you are

Louise i'm sorry?

Billy he's got a power over ya

Louise don't be daft

Billy no i'm telling ya

  Louise puts down the iron and stares at Billy.

Louise alright billy

  Billy is silent

what's all this about?

Billy you tell me

Louise tell you *what*?

Billy tell me where you did it

  Louise looks shocked.

was it on the settee?

  Louise is silent.

the ironing board?

  Louise is silent.

or was it in stan's bed?

  Louise smirks.

Louise you're mad you are

Billy i'm round the bend

Louise i dunno where you get these notions

Billy i wonder

Louise you've a flipping nerve above all else coming here screaming the odds it's enough to put me off my dinner

Billy what you having?

Louise yorkshire pudding

Billy midweek?

Louise looks indignant.

Louise yeh

Billy with beef?

Louise nods.

Louise for stan yeh

Billy that's nice

Louise his special treat

Billy why what's he done?

Louise nothing

Billy i see

Louise what?

Billy you feeling guilty are you?

Louise no

Billy sneers.

Billy you're a disgrace

Louise i've *told* you

Billy gets up and pours himself a refill. Louise watches him.

Billy he was stan's best man

Louise smirks.

Louise tell me about it

Billy what?

Louise he never stops saying

Billy i was well gutted

Louise raises her eyebrows.

Louise you fancied your chances?

Billy we all did i imagine

Louise there can only be one billy

Billy not so i saw a film where this chap chose *all* his mates

Louise did he?

Billy it was very civil

Louise i like a soppy film i do

Billy it weren't soppy lou it extolled the virtues of cameraderie

Billy points at Louise.

there's a difference

Louise i see

Billy he didn't wanna put his eggs in one basket

Louise why's that?

Billy lest he was having omelettes for breakfast

Louise looks cautious.

Louise how cautious

Billy well you have to be in this day and age

Louise and why?

Billy b/cos in every basket there's always a wrong'un

Louise and that's tommy is it?

Billy if you like

Louise i thought so

Billy points at Louise.

Billy there's two types of person walk this earth louise

Louise sighs.

Louise oh not this again

Billy the tommys of this world and the stans

Louise he's the right one

Billy a bit soft perhaps

Louise soft?

Billy easily fooled

Louise that's true

Billy what?

Louise shakes her head.

Louise i've had the wool over his eyes so long i don't believe it myself sometimes i mean there's me seeing his best mate and he utterly clueless it's a mystery but then he works so hard as you said i shouldn't be surprised i mean he can't keep tabs on me all day not from the office and why should he he's no cause to suspect he comes home his food's ready the washing the ironing he must think i'm cooped up in this miserable flat on my own!

Billy he knows you see me

Louise but that don't bother him

Billy why not

Louise he may be soft billy but he's not *that* daft

Billy nods.

Billy i see

Louise he probably *pities* me that's the funny bit he works his balls off for our future and i'm cavorting with tommy his best mate

Billy despite my efforts

Louise are you jealous?

Billy looks taken aback.

Billy of course

Louise you wanna fuck me too is that what this is about?

Billy peers at Louise up and down.

Billy many's the time i've gone to bed with *you* in my thoughts louise

Billy nods.

many's the time

Louise frowns.

Louise i don't fancy your chances

Billy no?

Louise there's one thing you can never buy billy

Billy are you sure i've plenty on me

Louise you can keep it

Billy so how does tommy pay lou?

Louise in his own way

Billy yeh?

Louise one you can never match

Billy not with cash?

Louise sniggers.

Louise i don't think so

Billy nods.

Billy he always was a mean bastard

Louise oh no billy he's very giving very giving he is

Billy i bet he is

Louise bites her bottom lip and smiles naughtily. Billy slaps her hard on the cheek.

bitch

Louise shrieks in pain. She goes to the floor. Billy kicks her hard in the midriff. She shrieks again. He stares down at her weeping. He downs his drink. Checks his watch. Collects his coat. Walks towards the door.

give stan my regards

Billy walks off. He is heard leaving the flat off-stage. Louise continues to lie in a heap weeping. Eventually she dries her eyes and gets up. She checks her face in the mirror. Cream appears and she rubs it on. She picks up the scattered notes and stuffs them in her pockets. She sees the tailor's box. Stares at it. Opens it. Pulls back the tissue paper. Looks inside. Pulls out the dress. It is the same colour as Billy's suit. She holds it out and looks at it. She holds it up against her body and looks at it in the mirror. From the front. From the sides. She hears someone enter the flat off-stage. She starts. Stuffs the dress back in the box. Stuffs the box under one of the sofa cushions. Stan walks on taking off his overcoat. Same colour suit as previous scene.

Stan hello love

Louise stan

Stan was that billy i saw driving off?

Louise yeh

Stan i called after him he didn't stop what did he want?

Louise explaining

Stan he didn't wait for me?

Louise he was pushed he said to send his regards

Stan nods.

Stan what did you say?

Louise my mind weren't for changing

Stan good for you love

Louise he weren't best pleased

Stan fuck him

Stan walks towards Louise.

Louise how was work?

Stan fine

Stan pecks Louise on the head. He sees her cheek and holds it up.

what's that?

Louise what?

Stan you look a bit red

Louise it's my rash i put some cream on it

Stan it's come up proper

Louise let's have a look

Louise looks at her cheek in the mirror.

Stan you know lou i'm glad you came round about tommy i was thinking of it today

Louise is silent.

i mean billy's alright

Louise is silent.

but he's tainted

Louise how dya mean?

Stan he has a mean streak trust me i found something out about him

Louise when?

Stan yesterday down the pub . . . something from years back

Louise what?

Stan nothing

Louise sighs.

Louise oh i give up

Stan are you alright love?

Louise i'm fine

Stan no i'd be wary of him lou but then i can't say that can i you see a side i don't and he you by all accounts

Louise's face drops. She turns to face Stan.

Louise has he said something?

Stan frowns.

Stan nah

Stan points at Louise.

no he did in actual fact

Louise what?

Stan he said joey was slow

Louise looks relieved.

Louise is that all?

Stan he's not lou he's shrewder than ya credit

Louise dya reckon?

Stan i do take yesterday

Louise what happened?

Stan i tell the boys my rod stewart tale you know the one where . . .

Louise yeh i know

Stan yeh course you do . . . sorry . . . anyway joey already knew it so he told em who said it

Louise when?

Stan firstly

Louise and who did?

Stan my dad

Louise stares at Stan.

Louise your dad?

Stan and they didn't get it

Louise get what?

Stan in fact *i* hadn't even got it till then!

Louise and that's important is it your dad telling you?

Stan of *course* it is that's the whole fucking point but it's lost on billy

Stan taps his temple.

he's the one who's slow i tell ya

   Louise looks bemused.

Louise he must be if he didn't get that

Stan anyway now i'm gonna tell *my* kids

   Louise looks startled.

Louise what?

   Stan raises his hand.

Stan *when* we have em i mean *if* we have em i'm not saying we *will* i'm saying *if* we do

Louise that might be sooner than you think

Stan what?

Louise i'm pregnant

   Stan stares at Louise. Long and hard.

Stan you never are?

   Louise nods.

Louise i'm afraid so

   Stan stares at Louise. Long and hard.

Stan well sit down for christ sake!

Louise what?

Stan take the weight off your feet!

   Stan drags Louise onto the sofa.

fucking hell

   Stan pulls off her slippers and puts her feet up. He stares at her.

that better?

Louise great

Stan now dya need something?

Louise looks surprised.

Louise what?

Stan nods.

Stan yeh

Louise oh i'd love a cup of tea

Stan walks towards the door. He checks.

Stan is that okay i mean ain't tea got caffeine?

Louise i believe so

Stan has an idea.

Stan i'll check the ingredients

Stan walks off. Louise gazes at the box. Stan walks on waving a box of PG Tips.

it ain't *got* any flaming ingredients!

Louise you don't say

Stan it's just *tea* for fuck sake what the *fuck's* this fucking world fucking *coming* to for crying out loud!?

Stan has an idea.

i'll get you a nice glass of water just calm down will ya

Stan walks off. Walks back on.

here lou dya think we should get that bottled water i mean those pipes ain't the cleanest by a long stretch

Louise stands.

Louise that's it!

Stan what?

Louise you're getting on my *wick* stan i'm pregnant i ain't *sick*!

Stan holds up his hands.

Stan okay for fuck sake calm down you'll wake the kid

Louise sighs.

shit!

Stan shakes his head.

wait till the boys hear this

Louise glares at Stan.

Louise is that all you can think of?

Stan looks bashful.

Stan no of course not

Louise you've not even said you're pleased

Stan opens his arms and smirks.

Stan what kinda question's that?

Louise i dunno

Stan here you sure you ain't mistaken?

Louise it's a fact

Stan shakes his head.

Stan well fancy that who'd have thought it hey?

Louise and why not?

Stan we've hardly been at it like rabbits lately

Louise stan

Stan well it's *true* you've hardly fancied it

Louise we did it that time

Stan thinks back.

Stan once

Louise well that's all it takes

Stan when you think of what we was like it coulda happened before . . . here i thought you was protected?

Louise so did i

Stan smirks.

Stan it's funny innit?

Louise what is?

Stan nature's way

Louise it's a sign that's what it is what with us moving and buying the bistro

Stan points at Louise.

Stan they say things come in threes don't they?

Louise you see

Stan here you don't think it's triplets do ya?

Louise don't be daft

They chuckle together.

Stan blimey

Louise they'll be three of the little lasses

Stan raises his hand.

Stan er excuse me

Louise what?

Stan they might be boys

Louise frowns.

Louise nah not these

Stan why not?

Louise a mother knows

Stan does she?

Louise it's biological anyroad

Stan what is?

Louise *all* my family are girls

Stan who?

Louise well my mum and *her* mum

Stan your auntie

Louise exactly

Stan but not your uncle

Louise no but he dresses up

Stan looks shocked.

Stan what?

Louise stan you're not to say nothing it's a secret

Stan i bet it is

Louise auntie may'd kill me

Stan so how dya know?

Louise i caught him at it

Stan when?

Louise when i was five

Stan what did he say?

Louise he was speechless

Stan i'm not surprised

Louise he was in her best frock as well

Stan looks shocked.

Stan no?

Louise nods.

uncle bert?

They laugh together.

i thought he was a normal fella?

Louise there you go

Stan and to think

Louise what?

Stan i played snooker with him

Louise stan you won't say nothing will ya?

Stan nods.

Stan well billy's right about one thing i'll say that

Louise what?

Stan it *is* a crazy world

Louise i suppose

Stan raises his hand.

Stan listen lou i don't care what ours is as long as he ain't a spurs fan

Louise what?

Stan a bender a cross-dresser whatever i can hack that but if he supports the yids

Stan points at Louise.

there'll be ructions i tell ya

Louise smiles.

Louise come here you daft thing

Stan walks up to Louise. They hug and kiss. He holds her head up.

Stan how come you never told me?

Louise you was working

Stan you coulda rung

Louise i wanted to digest it

Stan why?

Louise well when the doctor told me i just felt numb stan

Stan what did he say?

Louise he said you're pregnant

Stan what just like that!?

Louise yeh

Stan shakes his head.

Stan fucking hell

Louise what?

Stan modern science

Louise i just sat there staring i think he thought i was on drugs

Stan why?

Louise he was looking at me funny

Stan he fancies you that's what it is

Louise looks bemused.

Louise doctor patel?

Stan he was admiring your 'incandescent beauty'

Louise looks bemused.

Louise do what?

Stan it's one of tommy's

Louise anyhow i couldn't help thinking

Stan back?

Louise that's right

Stan that's typical of you lou it's time you started
thinking *forward* i mean things are on the *up* ain't they?

Louise i suppose

Stan of *course* they are what's *wrong* with you?

Louise nothing

Stan you seem a bit . . .

Stan checks.

Louise what?

Stan i dunno

Louise you dream of days like this when you're young

Stan do you?

Louise nods.

what?

Louise being married

Stan oh that

Louise getting pregnant . . . you wonder how it'll all pan out . . . *if* it'll all pan out . . . what kinda life you'll have . . . what kinda fella . . . if he'll love ya

Stan of *course* i do

Louise you dream of going away with him

Stan where?

Louise anywhere . . . wherever . . . somewhere hot . . . costa brava . . . just the two of ya decked out in the sun rubbing oil on each other like you see couples do when you're young and you look at couples . . . you think that'll be *me* one day that will i'll have a fella just *like* that who wipes the sand off me and fetches tall drinks from the bar . . . that'll be *me* . . . and we'll fly back and scurry home and put on the telly and i'll make a pot of tea for everyone not just us but all our friends who've come to visit not just *his* friends neither *mine* too *both* our friends they'll be friends with each *other* and we'll tell em of our stay and show off our tans and i'll make a nice pot of proper tea with a tea cosy and we'll settle back and watch a film perhaps

Louise's face drops.

or a game show

Louise has an idea.

or *play* a game even

Stan looks bemused.

Stan play one?

Louise yeh when did we last do that?

Stan we don't *play* games for christ sake we're married

Louise that's what marriage is all *about* i thought

Stan nods.

Stan when you was young yeh

Louise frowns.

Louise i suppose

Stan shakes his head.

Stan listen lou you wanna stop that i've told ya

Louise what?

Stan harking back to the past i mean look at what we've got hey

Stan opens his arms.

who'd have thought?

Stan opens his arms further.

a business

Stan nods at her belly.

a family

Stan points at her belly.

you see that kid?

Louise yeh

Stan it was made in england

Louise what?

Stan nods.

Stan it was made in fucking england

Louise of *course* it was

Stan shakes his head.

Stan i tell ya i love this country lou i won't slag it like billy i don't care *what* happens

Stan smells the air.

oh that smells good what is it?

Louise roast

Stan rubs his tummy.

Stan lovely

Louise i'll fetch it

Louise walks off. Stan goes straight for the drinks and pours himself a large scotch. He downs it in one and pours another. He sits on the sofa. Picks up the phone. Dials.

Stan here tommy call us back i got news

Stan starts to put the phone down then checks.

it's stan

Stan starts to put the phone down then checks.

i'm gonna be a dad you cunt

Stan starts to put the phone down then checks.

i'm gonna be a fucking dad!

Stan starts to put the phone down then checks.

don't say nothing i want it to be a surprise

Stan starts to put the phone down then checks.

i'll announce it at the do just play dumb

Stan starts to put the phone down then checks.

don't tell lou neither she doesn't know

Stan starts to put the phone down then checks.

i mean she knows she's *pregnant* she just doesn't know
i'm gonna *announce* it

Stan starts to put the phone down then checks.

she dunno *you* know neither so whatever you do don't
let on don't even *talk* to her i mean you can *talk* to her
don't *mention* it if you *ignore* she might suspect you
dopey cunt use your fucking loaf for once hello . . . ?
tommy . . . you're home . . . what?

Stan looks bemused.

edward . . . ? are you sure?

Stan shakes his head.

i dunno tommy it's a bit early . . . what?

Stan hears Louise approaching.

listen i gotta go

*Stan gently puts the phone down. He starts taking off
his shoes. Louise walks on holding two plates and
cutlery. The towel around her head has gone. Her hair
is dyed a bright and bold colour. Stan loosens his tie
and undoes his top shirt buttons. Louise hands him
his plate.*

ta love

*Stan puts the plate on his lap and looks at it: roast
beef, spuds, the works. He licks his lips and nods.*

handsome

*Stan tucks into his food and gazes at the box. He
doesn't see Louise's hair. He gasps. His mouth full.*

delicious

*Louise sits down beside Stan. On top of the tailor's
box. Her plate has far less: Yorkshire pudding and*

veg. Stan shakes his head. His mouth full.

you can't beat sunday roast we should do this at the
bistro

.

Stan makes a banner with his hand.

sunday roast 'every day of the week'

Louise picks at her food.

we're gonna make a proper go of this bistro

*Stan points his fork at her belly. His eyes fixed on the
TV.*

and when we're old we'll pass it on to our edward

Louise stares at Stan.

Louise edward?

Stan nods.

Stan yeh

Stan stuffs another forkful in his mouth.

'little eddie'

*Louise picks up the remote control. Flicks through the
channels.*

Louise we still want foreign food mind

Stan of course we do

Louise tortellini and asparagus

Stan definitely

Louise finds her preferred show.

we just won't neglect our traditional clientele

Louise puts down the remote control.

Louise fine

Stan stares at his next forkful and nods.

Stan fucking blinding

They gaze at the TV eating.

The End.

Discover the brightest and best in fresh theatre writing with Faber's new StageScripts

Sweetheart by Nick Grosso   0571 17967 3

Mules by Winsome Pinnock   0571 19022 7

The Wolves by Michael Punter   0571 19302 1

Gabriel by Moira Buffini   0571 19327 7

Skeleton by Tanika Gupta   0571 19339 0

The Cub by Stephanie McKnight   0571 19381 1

Fair Game by Rebecca Prichard   0571 19476 1
(a free adaptation of **Games in the Backyard** by Edna Mazya)

Crazyhorse by Parv Bancil   0571 19477 X

Sabina! by Chris Dolan   0571 19590 3

I Am Yours by Judith Thompson   0571 19612 8

Been So Long by Che Walker   0571 19650 0

Yard Gal by Rebecca Prichard   0571 1959 1

Sea Urchins by Sharman Macdonald   0571 19695 0

Twins by Maureen Lawrence   0571 20065 6

Real Classy Affair by Nick Grosso   0571 19592 X

Skinned by Abi Morgan   0571 20007 9

Down Red Lane by Kate Dean   0571 20070 2

Dogs Barking by Richard Zajdlic   0571 20006 0

All Faber *StageScripts* are priced at £4.50.
If you cannot find them stocked at your local bookshop please contact Faber Sales Department on 0171 465 0045